The LITTLE ROCK NINE and SCHOOL DESEGREGATION

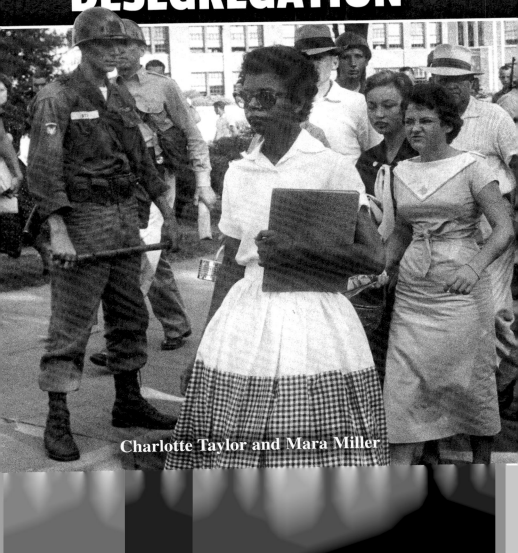

Charlotte Taylor and Mara Miller

Published in 2016 by Enslow Publishing, LLC
101 W. 23rd Street, Suite 240, New York, NY 10011

Cataloging-in-Publication Data

Taylor, Charlotte.

The Little Rock Nine and school desegregation / by Charlotte Taylor and Mara Miller.

p. cm. — (Our shared history)

Includes index.

ISBN 978-0-7660-7010-3 (library binding)

1. School integration — Arkansas — Little Rock — History — 20th century — Juvenile literature. 2. African Americans — Education — Arkansas — Little Rock — History — 20th century. 3. African American students — Arkansas — Little Rock — History — 20th century — Juvenile literature. I. Taylor, Charlotte. II. Miller, Mara. III. Title.

LC214.23.L56 T39 2016

379.2'630976773—d23

Printed in the United States of America

To Our Readers: We have done our best to make sure all Web site addresses in this book were active and appropriate when we went to press. However, the author and the publisher have no control over and assume no liability for the material available on those Web sites or any Web sites they may link to. Any comments or suggestions can be sent by e-mail to customerservice@enslow.com.

Portions of this book originally appeared in the book *School Desegregation and the Story of the Little Rock Nine*.

CONTENTS

Protestors voice their opposition to the integration of Little Rock Central High School.

The First Morning

"I had never seen such raw anger up close before. And this was directed at me. For what? Because I wanted to go to school?"[1]

—Carlotta Walls LaNier

Arkansas in the 1950s was a divided state. This division was based on one factor: the color of a person's skin. Blacks and whites did not eat together. They did not use the same restroom. They did not drink from the same water fountain. And they did not attend the same schools. But in 1957, nine brave young people stepped up and challenged that division. In doing so, they became pioneers in a movement to break down racial barriers throughout the South.

In 1954, the United States Supreme Court ruled that segregation in schools based on race was unconstitutional. Segregation means separation. The US Supreme Court is the highest court in the United States. This decision meant keeping black students out of schools attended by whites was illegal. In 1957, that ruling would be tested at a high school in Little Rock, Arkansas. For the first time in history, black students would walk through Central High School's stone and marble halls to attend classes.

Many people were unhappy with the Supreme Court's decision. In the 1950s, racism was widespread. This was especially true in southern states where enslaved Africans had once been used for labor. Racism is a belief that certain people are inferior based on physical features such as skin or hair color. Racist groups such as the Ku Klux Klan (KKK) used their belief in white supremacy to justify horrible crimes, including murder.

Most black families celebrated the Court's decision. But many were nervous. They worried that the desegregation would result in revenge from white people. They were afraid that they would lose their jobs. Or worse, they were afraid of mob violence against black people. They had reason to be afraid. Lynching happened too often in the Deep South. Lynching is killing somebody accused of a crime without a fair trial. Usually the victim is hung from a tree. Most lynching happened to black men.

In spite of their families' concerns, some black students spent the summer preparing to attend Central High that fall. It's not easy to enter a new school. And the students knew that starting this new school would be even more difficult. They attended numerous meetings and interviews. They were told how to behave and what to expect. School officials

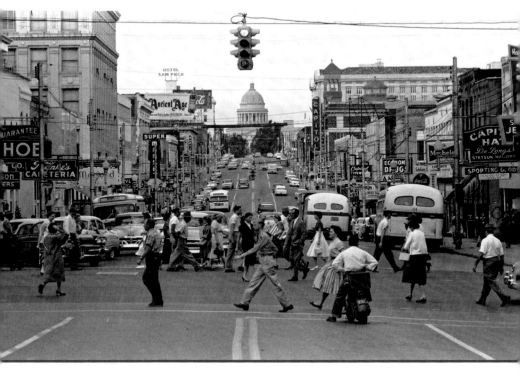

Little Rock is the capital of Arkansas and was considered by many to be a good place to begin integration.

actually tried to discourage the students from making the transfer. Despite their fears, the students were excited.

An Alarming Confrontation

Elizabeth Eckford, one of the black students, pressed the black and white skirt she had sewn for the first day of school. The television blared in the background. Elizabeth's mother told her to turn it off. She was too worried to listen to anymore news. Two nights

The Lynching of Emmett Till

On August 28, 1955, Emmett Till, a fourteen-year-old black boy, walked into a small grocery store in Money, Mississippi. Reports of what happened in the store differ, but some say that Till whistled at the white female owner of the store.[2] Several nights later, the woman's husband and another man kidnapped Till, beat and shot him, and threw him in a river.

Tens of thousands attended Till's funeral. His mother had asked that the casket be left open so that everyone could see how viciously Till had been attacked. Many newspapers and magazines covered the story and soon there was a large public outcry calling for justice for Emmett Till. At the trial, the two men were found not guilty of murder. They later admitted that they had murdered Till.

Till's story shone a spotlight on race relations in the South, and outraged many Americans, both black and white. The brutality of his murder and the lack of justice for his murderers helped to fuel the growing civil rights movement.

before, the governor of Arkansas had called out the National Guard. He had said they were there to keep the peace, but few people knew what their orders actually were. People wondered if they would protect the black students or keep them from entering the school. Elizabeth's dad paced with a sad and nervous expression. But Elizabeth was confident. She boarded a city bus and rode to Central High.

When Elizabeth got off the bus, she encountered a mob of people. She had not heard about a plan for the new black students to meet at the corner of Twelfth and Park streets. Instead she headed for the front of the school. She was nervous but not afraid. She was certain the guardsmen would protect her if the crowd got out of control.

At one point, she tried to pass a line of soldiers to get into the school. They would not let her through. Then one of the guards pointed across the street. Elizabeth thought he meant she should cross the street and go to the main entrance. She crossed and continued to walk.

The crowd followed behind her. The people moved like a single organism. They began shouting and calling Elizabeth names. They yelled, "Go home before you get hurt, nigger" and "Why don't you go back to the . . . jungle!"[3]

Elizabeth kept her head held high and walked until she was standing in front of the main door. She looked at the school surrounded by the National Guard. It was very big. The main building was more than two blocks long and contained one hundred classrooms.

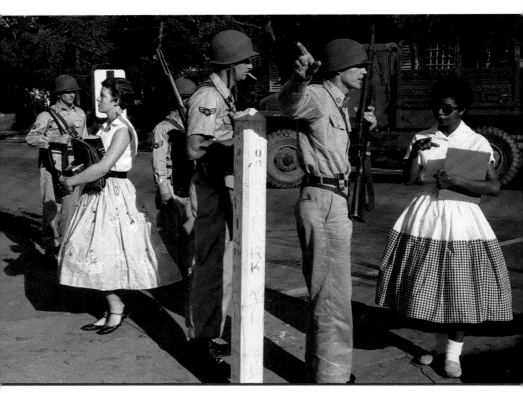

Elizabeth Eckford, right, is turned away by Arkansas National Guardsmen as she approaches Little Rock Central High.

Statues of Greek goddesses decorated the entry. The campus was four square blocks.

Summoning courage, Elizabeth tried to follow a white student inside. The soldiers closed ranks. They would not let her through. When she tried to squeeze past again, the soldiers raised their bayonets. The guardsmen were not there to protect the students or stop any violence. They were there to stop the black students from entering the school.

Elizabeth started to panic. Fear rose as the crowd moved closer. Someone shouted: "Lynch her!"[4] Elizabeth held her books and looked for a friendly face. When she thought she found one, the woman spat on her. She saw a bus stop a block away and began walking toward it. The crowd was at her heels shouting insults. Someone yelled, "Get a rope and drag her over to this tree."[5]

Keeping her eyes forward, Elizabeth made it to the bus stop's bench. A *New York Times* reporter sat next to her and put his arm around her. Tears were streaming from under her dark glasses. The reporter lifted her chin, "Don't let them see you cry," he told her.[6] Grace Lorch, a white professor's wife, sat on the other side of her.

Lorch yelled at the mob, "Leave this child alone. . . . Six months from now, you will hang your heads in shame."[7] Members of the crowd yelled insults at Lorch and told her to leave. They did not want her to protect Elizabeth. When Lorch tried to call a cab for Elizabeth, members of the crowd blocked Lorch's access to a phone.

Fortunately, the bus came. Lorch boarded with Elizabeth and sat next to her. She tried to talk to Elizabeth, but the girl was too shaken to answer. Elizabeth rode to where her mother worked at a school for the blind. She ran inside and up the stairs. When Elizabeth saw the fear in her mother's expression, all she could do was hug her mother and cry.

The LITTLE ROCK NINE and SCHOOL DESEGREGATION

An Angry Mob

Melba Pattillo, another one of the new black students, drove with her mother to the school. They parked several blocks away from the arranged meeting place. The mob made it impossible for them to get any closer. As Melba and her mother walked, they looked for friendly faces but did not see any. Then they saw Elizabeth trying to enter the school. They watched as the guardsmen repeatedly blocked her entrance. Melba wanted to help Elizabeth but could not push her way through the crowd. She and her mother prayed for Elizabeth's safety as the crowd began to chant "Get her, Get the nigger out of there."[8]

The crowd was becoming more aggressive. Melba and her mother sensed that they were in a dangerous situation. They tried to turn around and quietly walk back to their car. But two white men noticed and started to chase them. Another white man joined in, carrying a rope. The men were violent and angry. Melba got the car keys from her mother. Melba's mother told her to leave without her if she had to. Melba was able to get both her mother and herself in the car before gunning it in reverse to make an escape.

No Entrance

The other black students were jostled and shoved as they made their way toward the school. For safety's sake, they walked between four ministers—two white and two black. The crowd jeered. Reporters asked the students questions, and photographers snapped their pictures.

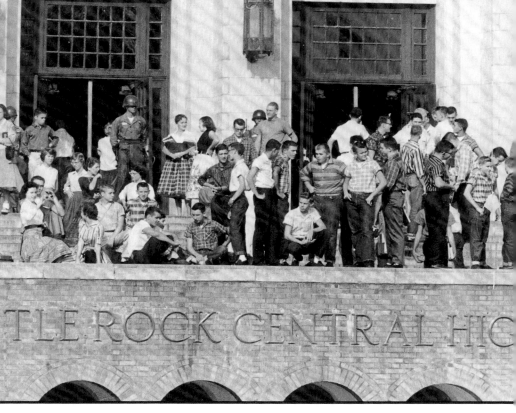

National guardsmen and a group of white students stand in front of Central High School in Little Rock, Arkansas, to block any African-American students from entering.

When the students reached the school, it was the same as it had been with Elizabeth. The guardsmen would not let them enter. One of the ministers asked a captain of the guardsmen why. The officer answered that they were acting on orders from Arkansas Governor Orval Faubus.

The Fight for Equality in Schools

During slave times in America, most southern states had laws against teaching slaves to read or write. There were several reasons for these laws. If a slave could read books, he might read about places where all people were free. With his new knowledge, he might question what he was told by his owners. And if a slave could write, she might correspond with others and organize an escape. She might even forge traveling documents to aid in that escape. Knowledge was power, so slave owners wanted to keep their slaves ignorant.

After the Civil War ended in 1865, Congress passed the Thirteenth Amendment, which abolished, or ended, slavery in the United States. Congress then passed two amendments, or additions, to the Constitution to protect the rights of African Americans. The Fourteenth Amendment (1868) guaranteed citizenship and equal protection under the law to anyone born or naturalized in the United States. This was very important to the newly freed slaves who would now be American citizens. This amendment prevented states from making or enforcing laws that reduced the privileges or protections granted to citizens. No state could take away life, liberty, or property without due process of law. And all citizens were granted equal protection under the law. The Fifteenth Amendment (1870) granted black men the right to vote. This amendment says that the right to vote "cannot be denied or abridged by race, color, or previous condition of servitude." (White and black women would not get to vote until 1920.)

Congress also created the Freedmen's Bureau to help the newly freed slaves. Most former slaves had little education and no money or property. One of the bureau's responsibilities and its biggest success was education.

Former Slaves Go to School

The newly freed slaves knew the importance of education to equality. One Freedmen's Bureau agent reported in 1865 that when he told three thousand newly freed slaves they would be educated, "They fairly jumped and shouted in gladness."[1]

Missionaries taught children by day and adults by night. "I never before saw children so eager to learn," said Charlotte Forten. She was the daughter of the wealthy African-American shipyard owner James Forten. She taught on an island off the coast of South Carolina. "Coming to school is a constant delight and recreation to them," she wrote. "They come here as

An 1866 poster attacks the Freedmen's Bureau for supporting former slaves.

other children go to play. The older ones, during the summer, work in the fields from early morning until eleven or twelve o'clock, and then come into school, after their hard toil in the hot sun, as bright and anxious to learn as ever."[2] A newly freed slave said he would make sure his children went to school because he considered "education [the] next best thing to liberty."[3]

Schools opened wherever there was space—sometimes in tents, shanties, barns, and even outside at open meetings. As more schools opened, both black and white students began taking advantage of the free educational opportunities. Over time, a public school system developed in the South.

The Jim Crow Laws

Many white southerners felt that the three amendments protecting the newly freed slaves were forced on their states after the Civil War. Many were still angry that slavery had been abolished. As time passed, the northern states grew less interested in the rights of African-American citizens and more interested in the growing economy. The rights granted and protected by the Fourteenth and Fifteenth amendments were chipped away in the South by state and local laws.

These laws, known as "Jim Crow laws," were enacted in many southern states. Jim Crow was a theater character made up by a white man to make fun of blacks. Jim Crow laws were designed to keep African Americans from gaining true equality. Blacks and whites were separated by race in railroad cars, schools, restaurants, parks, theaters, churches, and even in bathrooms and at drinking fountains. The best facilities were saved for white people.

Many southern states effectively took away African Americans' right to vote. The Fifteenth Amendment says no state can prohibit voting by race. So the white politicians used property ownership, literacy tests, and poll taxes as a requirement for voting. Most slaves had not been educated and very few owned property or had the money to pay the tax on voting. When African Americans did meet the requirements, state voting officials often made the questions they asked

Jim Crow laws would not allow whites and blacks to eat, travel, worship, or even watch movies together.

impossible to answer. One question that a voting official in the South asked an African-American man was: "How many bubbles are there in a cake of soap?" When the man did not have an answer, he was told to go home.[4]

Separate but Equal

In the 1890s, Homer Plessy challenged these laws. Plessy, a black man, entered a railcar marked whites-only. When he refused to leave, he was arrested. He sued the state of Louisiana, asserting that the separation marked him as inferior. At issue was the meaning of the Fourteenth Amendment.

His case went to the US Supreme Court. In 1896, the Court handed down the majority decision. It stated that while the Fourteenth Amendment's objective had been to enforce equality between the two races before the law, "it could not have been intended to abolish distinctions based upon color, or to enforce social, as distinguished from political equality, or a commingling of the two races upon terms unsatisfactory to either."[5] They had ruled that segregation was legal.

Only one associate justice disagreed. Justice John Marshall Harlan foresaw the terrible consequences. He said that "our Constitution is color-blind" and that "the interests of both [races] require that the common government of all shall not permit the seeds of race hate to be planted under the sanction of law."[6] But he was only one of nine justices.

Unfair Treatment

Throughout the South, the separate facilities were rarely, if ever, equal. The drinking fountains marked for blacks did not work as well and were sometimes dirty, while the better water fountains would say whites-only. African Americans were forced to sit in the backs of buses. Many stores and restaurants were off-limits to them as well. Those that were open to black customers would serve all their white customers first, and some would only serve black customers out the back door. Whites-only waiting rooms in railway stations would be bigger and have more seats. Sometimes the waiting rooms for African Americans would not even have heat.

The LITTLE ROCK NINE and SCHOOL DESEGREGATION

White citizens often became enraged when these unfair rules were broken. Melba Pattillo, one of the black students who tried to attend Central High, remembers being an eight-year-old and having to go to the bathroom. The bathroom for white people was much closer. (They were usually closer. There were more whites-only bathrooms, and they were in central locations.) Her curiosity combined with the urgent need sent her running into the forbidden restroom.

She barely had time to notice how much nicer, bigger, and cleaner the whites-only bathroom was compared to those she usually used. But she did notice. It was as pretty as she had imagined. The women inside the bathroom screamed at her and called her "nigger." They ordered her to get out. But it was too late. She had already sat down to go to the bathroom. When she finished, the police were waiting for her outside the bathroom door. Her grandmother spent over an hour explaining to the police before they would let them go.

Fighting Back

During World War II (1939–1945), both black and white soldiers risked their lives and fought for freedom. Although the black soldiers had fought as hard and risked as much as their white counterparts, they were not considered equal. They had witnessed the evils of racism overseas in Adolf Hitler's regime, only to find them again at home. This made a lot of the black veterans angry. They had risked their lives

White facilities were usually of higher quality and were better maintained than black facilities.

for freedom in Europe. They were willing to risk them again for equality in the United States.

It had been nearly fifty years since the Supreme Court's *Plessy v. Ferguson* decision. The idea of "separate but equal" was firmly set in the laws of the southern states and the minds of many. Only the highest court in the nation could overturn the *Plessy v. Ferguson* decision. The Supreme Court changing one of its previous decisions is rare. But it was a different time and there were nine different justices on the Court.

The Plan

World War II had unsettled many white Americans as well. They also saw the racism that they hated

The LITTLE ROCK NINE and SCHOOL DESEGREGATION

in Germany reflected at home. In 1948, President Truman desegregated the military. The time was ripe for change and the National Association for the Advancement of Colored People (NAACP) had a plan.

The NAACP is an organization that fights to end racial discrimination. It began in response to a race riot in Springfield, Illinois. During the riot, eight African-American men died. Two thousand more African Americans left the city out of fear for their lives. Afterward, fifty-three mostly white social workers, educators, lawyers, and clergy members signed a letter attacking racism and defending the rights of black Americans. A year later, many of the signers joined and formed the organization.

In 1934, the NAACP hired Charles Hamilton Huston as full-time legal counsel. Huston had been a law professor at Howard University in Washington, DC. There, he taught his students to be the best attorneys they could be. He believed that the law was a powerful weapon that could help the disadvantaged. He carefully studied the rules of law and the court opinions of prior cases. Then he developed a legal plan for the NAACP. Instead of challenging the idea of having separate facilities, Huston would attack the unequal nature of them.

It was easy to prove that schools and other African-American facilities were inferior. Schools for African-American children were usually overcrowded. The buildings were often in poor condition and many did not have indoor plumbing. Black students were often bussed considerable distances even though a white school might be much closer. The all-black schools were often poorly equipped. Students might not have desks and the books were often the old and discarded copies from white schools. Author and historian, Richard Kluger, described one all-black junior high school's science lab as consisting of "a Bunsen burner and a bowl of goldfish."[7]

Huston hoped that if states had to provide truly equal facilities, the cost would be too high and the states would be forced to end segregation. He also hoped that by getting lower court rulings in the NAACP's favor, they would be able to prove that separate could never be equal.

Going to Court

At Howard University, Charles Huston taught a young attorney named Thurgood Marshall. Marshall was a star debater and Huston's best student. When Huston accepted the NAACP's job offer, he asked them to hire Marshall as well.

Huston and Marshall made an amazing legal team. One of their first victories was for Donald Murray. Murray was a black student who wanted to attend the University of Maryland's law school. Huston and Marshall argued that Murray could not get an equal education at Princess Anne Academy, the alternative school open to black students. Princess Anne Academy did not even have a law degree available. The court ruled in favor of Murray. The University of Maryland was forced to change its policies on race.

The LITTLE ROCK NINE and SCHOOL DESEGREGATION

Schools for black students often could not afford supplies like books or science equipment.

In 1938, Marshall took the reins from his mentor and became chief counsel of the NAACP's legal defense and education fund. During the next twelve years, he fought many legal battles. He was a talented attorney and won many cases including several that ended segregation in higher education. But Marshall had bigger goals. He wanted to "obtain full and complete integration of all students on all levels of public education without regard to race or color."[8]

In 1950, several court cases in the South challenged segregation in elementary schools. Marshall and other NAACP attorneys argued these cases in the lower courts of South Carolina, Kansas, Delaware, Virginia, and Washington, DC. The cases were appealed until they reached the US Supreme Court. There they were combined into one case. The names of the thirteen plaintiffs (the parents of the twenty children involved in the suit) were written alphabetically. The case name was too long and therefore shortened to *Brown* (the first name on the list) *v. Board of Education*. In December of 1952, the Supreme Court heard the first oral (spoken) arguments.

A Brilliant Argument

Marshall worried about the outcome of the *Brown v. Board of Education* case. People had risked time, money, security, and their very safety. People who were involved were often fired from their jobs, and sometimes their lives were threatened. Marshall knew he needed to move forward. But he worried that the families' sacrifice would be for nothing.

In court, Marshall argued that separate schools resulted in feelings of inferiority. He used new psychological evidence to show that black children were harmed by racial discrimination. Psychologist Kenneth Clark tested children's attitudes using dolls of different races. He found that black children, when asked which dolls were prettier or nicer, would generally point to the white dolls, indicating that the black dolls were less pretty or less nice. This showed that black children saw themselves as inferior to whites. It was evidence that discrimination was harming these children's ideas about themselves.

In oral arguments, Marshall challenged the idea that black and white children would have problems if schools were desegregated. "Everyone knows that is not true," he told the Court. "Those same kids in Virginia and South Carolina . . . they play in the streets together, they play on their farms together, they go down the road together, they separate to go to school, they come out of school and play ball together."[9]

Later in written arguments, Marshall argued that the only way that racial restrictions could be considered constitutional would be if the Court ruled that African Americans were inferior and therefore should be separated from other human beings. This put additional pressure on the Court to go beyond the historical and legal arguments and determine what was ethical or the right thing to do. With Marshall's powerful speeches, brilliant legal arguments, and flawless presentation (he would rather retype his work than let it have a typo), it was hard for anyone to say he was inferior.

The Decision

Although the individual school-discrimination cases began in 1950 and reached the Supreme Court in December 1952, it was not until 1954 that a decision was announced. In September 1953, Chief Justice Fred M. Vinson died. President Dwight D. Eisenhower appointed former California Governor Earl Warren to take his place. Vinson had believed in segregation. Justice Warren was against it.

Justice Marshall

As chief counsel for the NAACP, Thurgood Marshall was one of the most important civil rights activists of his time.

Marshall grew up in segregated Baltimore. His principal punished him by making him memorize parts of the US Constitution. By graduation, he knew the whole document by heart. He knew that some of the words he memorized did not fit with the racism and segregation he faced.

Thurgood's father, William Marshall, never told Thurgood to become a lawyer. But he turned him into one. "He did it by teaching me to argue, by challenging my logic on every point, by making me prove every statement I made," Marshall later recalled.[10]

Justice Thurgood Marshall

During his time with the NAACP, beginning in 1936, Marshall won twenty-seven out of thirty-two cases that went to the Supreme Court. In 1967, President Lyndon B. Johnson nominated Marshall for the US Supreme Court. Marshall, the Court's first African-American justice, served until 1991.

Thurgood Marshall died on January 24, 1993.

The LITTLE ROCK NINE and SCHOOL DESEGREGATION

When Warren took office, there were probably enough votes to overturn the *Plessy v. Ferguson* decision on a 5 to 4 vote. But Warren felt the Court needed to speak with one voice. He took every opportunity he had to talk to the four members who disagreed. By March, the votes were 8 to 1 to overturn. By May, it was unanimous.

On May 17, 1954, Warren read the decision:

> To separate [children] from others of similar age and qualifications solely because of their race generates a feeling of inferiority as to their status in their community that may affect their hearts and minds in a way unlikely to ever be undone. . . . [Therefore,] we conclude that in the field of public education the doctrine of "separate but equal" has no place.[11]

For Marshall, the only disappointment with the *Brown v. Board of Education* decision was that it had not set a date for integration. It took almost another year before the Court stated how the decision should be applied. This decision further disappointed Marshall. The decree stated that desegregation should take place "with all deliberate speed." The Court wanted to give schools time to prepare. But Marshall knew that the Court's language would give southern states time to delay.

In Little Rock, the school district announced that it would comply within five days of the decision. School superintendent Virgil Blossom proposed a plan for gradual desegregation starting at the high school level.

Some of the children involved in the *Brown v. Board of Education* case pose for a photo in 1953.

All-black schools would remain, but a small number of chosen students would be allowed into the all-white Central High School starting in 1957. Integration would then gradually move to the elementary schools in the following years until anyone who wished to transfer could.

Black families saw the "Blossom plan" as a way of stalling. The NAACP challenged the plan in court because it was too slow. But the court decided that the plan met the requirement of all deliberate speed.

The Little Rock Nine

"I began to feel as though we had formed some kind of group—an odd family of people with one goal: to get inside Central High and stay there for the school year."[1]

—Melba Pattillo Beals

Once the decision was made to send black students to all-white Central High School, the next question was: Who will go? Many students saw this event as an important opportunity. Initially, seventy or eighty students expressed an interest in transferring.[2] Following an in-depth screening process, the majority of students were ruled out. Some people questioned the methods used for screening, accusing the school of discouraging the students from transferring. The school defended itself, however, saying there were simply choosing the top students in order to ensure the success of the integration.

In the end, only seventeen students remained after the screening. Seven of them withdrew before school began. Another, Jane Hill, returned to the all-black school after being turned away from Central High on September 4. In all, nine students attended Central High. These nine students were on the battle lines of desegregation. Their intense experiences made them a sort of family. They became known as the Little Rock Nine.

Who They Were

Ernest Green was the oldest. He started Central High as a senior. His eyes were warm and he had an easy smile. His father's death in World War II had made him grow up early. Smart and well-spoken, he told his mother that he wanted to attend Central High. He felt that the *Brown* decision opened a window of opportunity for him to be a part of African-American history. He already knew that "if things were going to change, it wasn't going to be handed to [him]."[3] His mother pointed out the difficulty of entering a new school in his senior year. However, she said she would stand behind him.

Elizabeth Eckford was also determined to go to Central High. Her mother tried to delay registering her. She hoped Elizabeth would forget about it. But Elizabeth did not. After two weeks passed, she told her mother, "We're going to the school board office [to register] and we're going today."[4] Elizabeth was only fifteen years old and very shy by nature. But she

In 1958, the governor of New York W. Averell Harriman, grants awards to the Little Rock Nine for advancing the cause of equal rights. In the front row, from left to right: Minnijean Brown, Gloria Ray, Ernest Green, Carlotta Walls, and Melba Pattillo. In the back row, from left to right: Terrence Roberts, Elizabeth Eckford, Thelma Mothershed, and Jefferson Thomas.

wanted to be a lawyer. She thought attending Central High would help her become one.[5]

Melba Pattillo would enter Central High as a junior. She raised her hand on a whim when her teacher asked for students who wanted to transfer. She never discussed her interest with her family. They were surprised when they learned that she was assigned to Central High. Her father demanded that she not attend. His boss was threatening to fire him if she did. Her grandmother, however, believed that it was important for the black students to take a stand for equality.[6] Her Auntie Mae said that Melba "was just sassy enough to pull [integration] off."[7]

Minnijean Brown was a good friend of Melba's. They lived a block apart. Both loved to sing, and both were tall for their age. Minnijean's father wanted her to attend Central, but her mother was afraid for her safety. Minnijean was outgoing, friendly, and wanted to fit in. She had no problem expressing her emotions. Her temper, reasonable but quicker than the others, made her a target during the school year.

Jefferson Thomas would enter Central High as a sophomore. He had the type of subtle humor that made people laugh when they were not supposed to. Slim and athletic, he was a track star at his old school. He was also the student council president. He was willing to give those things up for the opportunities he felt that Central High School offered. Jefferson wanted to go to college and had dreams of greatness. Most of the black schools did not have college preparatory classes for his chosen interests.[8]

Thelma Mothershed was another determined student. At age sixteen, she was small and often pale due to a heart condition. Her parents worried that transferring to Central High would hurt her heart. They called a family meeting. Her two sisters, both in college, came home to discuss it. One of her sisters was the first African American to attend Enid University in Oklahoma. At the end of the family meeting, Thelma got her wish. She registered for Central High. The stress would prove hard on her heart. It would

The LITTLE ROCK NINE and SCHOOL DESEGREGATION

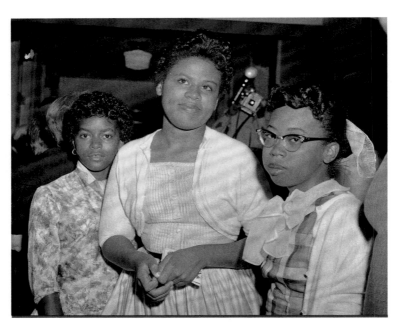

Minnie Brown (center) and Thelma Mothershed (right) wait in a corridor of the US Courthouse at Little Rock, where they were called to testifiy at a hearing on the integration problems at Central High School in 1957.

cause her to collapse during her first day in the school. But in spite of her heart condition, she would have near perfect attendance for the year.

Gloria Ray's father also had a heart condition. Gloria's mother was so worried about her husband's heart that she did not tell him about Gloria's transfer to Central High. He learned of it on the television the first day of school. He then offered to send Gloria to any private school of her choice. She told her dad that she loved him dearly and certainly would not do anything to impair his health. But quit Central High? No. That was something she could not do.

Terrence Roberts was fifteen and searching for a place where things were different. Like the others, he could not understand the hatred shown to him by white people he did not even know. When the school board came and asked who would be willing to enroll in Central High, Terrence raised his hand. He hoped that it would be the start of a positive change. He hoped that he would not have to leave Arkansas to find a place where he was not judged by the color of his skin. His parents supported his decision. With a pencil tucked behind his ear, he often hummed a cheerful tune. His funny and intelligent commentary would make his fellow students smile.

Carlotta Walls declared that she would attend Central High even if she had to go it alone.[9] She liked to swim, bowl, and play baseball. Rosa Parks, a civil rights leader who had refused to give up her seat on an Alabama bus to a white person, inspired Carlotta to get the best education she could. So, when her homeroom teacher passed around a paper for students to sign if they were interested in attending Central High, she wrote her name. Her parents supported her decision, but her young mother's hair turned almost white with worry during that first year.[10]

Rosa Parks Inspires a Movement

The Little Rock Nine were all familiar with the name Rosa Parks. The black seamstress from Montgomery, Alabama, was also the secretary for her local chapter of the NAACP. In December of 1955, Parks refused to move to the "colored" section of the bus so a white person could have her seat. She was then arrested for civil disobedience. Her act of defiance started the Montgomery Bus Boycott, in which black people across the city refused to ride the buses. The boycott lasted for over a year, until bus desegregation was finally declared unconstitutional by the Supreme Court.

Rosa Parks

Parks lost her job as a result of her actions, and she constantly received death threats. But she continued to speak out for racial equality and became a symbol of the civil rights movement.

Calling In the Troops

Daisy Bates was not a person who was afraid to speak her mind. As co-owner of a small newspaper, she spoke out whenever she saw racial injustice or violence. And as president of the Arkansas branch of the NAACP, she fought for the rights of African Americans across the state.

Daisy and her husband, L.C. Bates, often reported on instances of discrimination in their newspaper, the *Arkansas State Press*. They condemned police brutality against black citizens. They took up the cause of black World War II veterans who experienced racism and harassment. Reporting these truths sometimes resulted in advertisers pulling their money from the paper. Advertising is the life blood of a newspaper, and the *Arkansas State Press* was often low on funds. But the couple stuck to their beliefs and the paper survived.

The LITTLE ROCK NINE and SCHOOL DESEGREGATION

In her role as head of the state's NAACP, Bates was heavily involved in the planning of the desegregation at Central High School. She was aware of the risks involved but had no intention of backing down.

A few weeks before school started, Bates was listening to the news in her living room. A rock shattered her window. The rock came with a note that read: "Stone this time. Dynamite Next."[1]

Rumblings of Trouble

Throughout the summer, segregationists worked to stop integration from happening. A group called the Capital Citizen's Council purchased ads that encouraged people to "write, wire, or phone" Governor Faubus and tell him to stop the "race-mixing."[2] They hosted a dinner for three hundred segregationists, featuring Governor Marvin Griffin of Georgia. Speaking to the crowd, Griffin urged them to join his state in resisting integration. The crowd clapped and cheered.

Segregationists also tried to challenge the decision in court. On August 29, they asked Judge Murray O. Reed for an order to stop integration. Governor Faubus testified about a rumor that the white and black youths were forming gangs. He said he personally knew that "revolvers had been taken from Negro and white pupils." Judge Reed granted the injunction. Reporters investigated Governor Faubus's claim but did not find any evidence to verify it.[3]

That night, the segregationists celebrated. They drove around town blaring their horns, and yelling, "The Coons Won't Be Going to Central."[5] The NAACP

A Champion for Equal Rights

Daisy Gatson was seven years old when she first encountered the evils of racism. Her mother sent her to the store for pork chops. The butcher told her that "niggers have to wait 'til I wait on the white people."[4]

A year later, Daisy's mother was murdered while resisting rape by three white men. Daisy was filled with anger and hate. But she loved and admired her adoptive parents.

Daisy Gatson would grow up to become an integral part of the civil rights movement. She married a journalist named Lucious Christopher, also known as L.C., Bates. Together they published a newspaper that spoke out against the mistreatment of African Americans.

In 1952 Daisy Bates became the leader of the Arkansas branch of the NAACP. She continued working for the NAACP until 1972.

In 1962 she wrote a book about the Little Rock crisis called *The Long Shadow of Little Rock*. It was republished in 1986 and won the American Book Award.

Daisy Bates died in 1999 at the age of eighty-five.

filed a petition with Federal Judge Ronald N. Davies the next day. Judge Davies overrode Judge Reed's decision and ordered the school board to continue with integration.

Then on Labor Day weekend, as most of the Little Rock Nine were enjoying their last night before school with picnics and swimming, Governor Faubus prepared to address the state. Jefferson Thomas was visiting Daisy Bates at the time. Together, they wondered what Faubus would say.

"Is there anything they can do—now that they lost in court? Is there any way they can stop us from entering Central tomorrow morning?" Jefferson asked Bates.[6]

Bates did not think so. But at around 7:00 P.M., a newspaper reporter came to her door. He asked if she knew that the National Guard was surrounding the school. She did not. She and her husband quickly drove to Central High to see what was happening.

Army trucks and jeeps lined the street. Soldiers wearing helmets and carrying guns with bayonets were piling out of trucks and climbing the stairs in front of the school. It was almost too much to believe.

Daisy Bates rushed home to hear Governor Faubus's speech.

The Governor Takes a Stand

Governor Orval Faubus was tall and hawkish. His dark, thinning hair was slicked back in the style of the time. He wore a dark suit and dark tie. He had a way of making people feel that he was one of them.

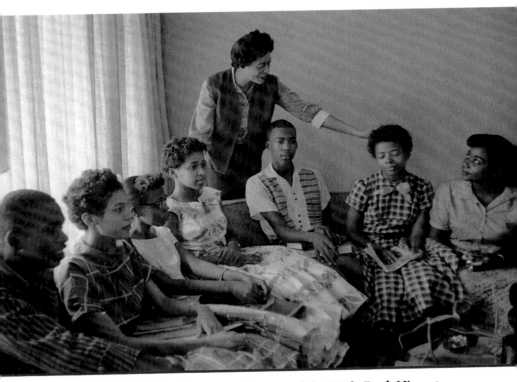

Daisy Bates (standing) talks with some of the Little Rock Nine at her home in Little Rock in October 1957.

He announced that knives and weapons were being purchased in alarming numbers. He said that caravans of white supremacists were coming to Little Rock. He predicted that "blood [would] run in the streets" if the African-American students attempted to start school the next day.[7]

> I must state here in all sincerity, that it is my opinion, yes, even a conviction, that it will not be possible to restore or to maintain order and protect the lives and property of the citizens if forcible integration is carried

out tomorrow in the schools of this community. . . . therefore . . . the schools in Pulaski County, for the time being, must be operated on the same basis as they have been operated in the past.[8]

In his speech, the governor was forbidding the nine students from entering Central High.

There is little evidence that there was a significant threat or that caravans of people were coming to the school before Faubus's interference. But his speech caused uproar and panic in both the black and white communities. As Melba Pattillo's grandmother said, "[Faubus] was stirring up trouble by talking about trouble."[9]

Faubus's speech gave many segregationists more confidence. They had reason to believe that the governor was on their side. Phones started ringing all around Little Rock. Some of the callers threatened the black students. One caller told Melba Pattillo that he knew her address and would be over to bomb the house. Another said, "Niggers don't belong in our schools. You-all are made for hanging."[10]

Melba's grandmother sat up all night with a shotgun. Melba wrote in her diary: "Maybe going to Central High isn't such a good idea after all. It's costing my family a lot of agony and energy. Will grandma always have to sit up guarding us?"[11]

An Uncertain Time

The parents of the Little Rock Nine contacted Daisy Bates. They wanted to know what the speech meant. They feared for their children's safety. The governor had said that "blood would run in the streets."[12]

Elizabeth Eckford's mother, Birdie, told Daisy Bates about seeing a lynch mob when she was a girl in 1927. She witnessed the mob dragging a black man down the street. The mob had later used church pews to burn the man's body. Bates tried to reassure Mrs. Eckford. There had been a lot of progress in Little Rock since 1927. Governor Faubus had said in his speech that the troops were there for protection. He had assured the people that the guardsmen were neither segregationist nor integrationist. They were soldiers with assigned tasks. The troops would protect the students, she reasoned.

The NAACP lawyers went back to Judge Ronald Davies, who was in charge of the Arkansas desegregation cases. The lawyers wanted to find out what they should do about the delay and the governor's statement. Judge Davies said that he was taking the governor at "face value."[13] The troops were there to protect citizens and property. He did not think they were there to stop desegregation. He told the NAACP and school officials that the students should start school the next morning.

The school superintendent Virgil Blossom spoke to the nine students and their parents. He asked that adults not be present the next day when the students

The LITTLE ROCK NINE and SCHOOL DESEGREGATION

Arkansas Governor Orval Faubus claimed that he called the troops to Central High School to protect the students.

came to school. He said it would be easier to protect them if they came alone.

Keeping the Students Safe

The idea of sending the students alone made Daisy Bates and some of the parents uneasy. Then a young reporter came to Daisy Bates's door. Sending those kids alone would be "murder," he told her. The crowd was growing and "they've gone mad."[14] Daisy Bates knew she had to keep the kids safe. She asked church ministers to walk with the children the next day. Surely the mob would not attack leaders of a church. The minister she spoke with said he would be there. But he did not know how many others would come.

Daisy Bates also called the police. She told an officer her concerns and what she had heard about the crowd. The officer promised to have a squad car near the school. But he would not be able to help after the students neared the school grounds. The police were forbidden to get close to the school as long as the troops were there.

Finally, Bates called the families. It was after 2:00 A.M. She told the students to meet at Twelfth and Park streets at 8:30 A.M., so they could walk with the church ministers. Bates was unable to speak with Elizabeth Eckford's family. The Eckfords did not have a phone in their home. By 3:00 A.M., Bates decided it would be best to tell Elizabeth in the morning. Exhausted, she went to sleep.

The next morning, Daisy and L. C. Bates drove to the meeting place. As they drove, they heard on the car radio that an African-American student was being mobbed in front of the school. Daisy Bates felt sick. It had to be Elizabeth. In the morning rush, Bates had forgotten to tell her about the plan to meet and walk as a group. Daisy Bates prayed for Elizabeth's safety as L.C. rushed to find her. She was relieved when L.C. came back and said that Elizabeth had safely boarded a bus. She was also thankful to see four ministers, two white and two black, waiting and willing to walk with the rest of the students.

The LITTLE ROCK NINE and SCHOOL DESEGREGATION

A Tense Wait

After the students were turned away, racial tension increased in Little Rock. The crowd around the school grew. The FBI investigated the governor's reports of potential violence. The US Attorney General Herbert Brownell asked for an injunction against the governor. This would be a legal order forcing the governor to stop interfering. A court date was set for September 20.

Until the court date, the Little Rock Nine had little choice but to wait. Most of them were confined to their homes. Their parents feared they would be attacked if seen outside. Their phones rang with threats. Melba's house was shot at. Her grandmother returned fire and scared the gunmen away.

The nine students tried to keep up with their schoolwork. Teachers at Central High sent them their assignments. Grace Lorch, the woman who had sat with Elizabeth on the bus bench, organized tutoring sessions. She and her husband held classes for the students at the local community college.

A Meeting With the President

Governor Faubus asked to see President Eisenhower. The president agreed to meet with Faubus. Eisenhower had not shown support for the *Brown v. Board of Education* decision. He did not believe laws should be forced on people from the top down. He was concerned that the Supreme Court had overstepped its bounds. He had even said that he could not imagine a situation that would cause him to send federal troops to enforce orders of a federal court. Eisenhower's

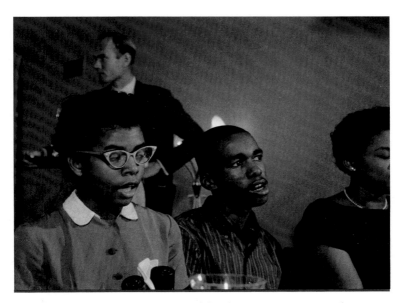

From left to right: Elizabeth Eckford, Ernest Green, and Minnie Jean Brown are seen at a dinner party in their honor at the home of a friend.

stance on the issue encouraged the segregationists. Many black leaders worried what the president and governor would decide behind closed doors without anyone representing African Americans.

However, Eisenhower was a man of duty. He told a friend in a letter the summer before the crisis that:

> There must be respect for the Constitution—
> which means the Supreme Court's interpretation of
> the Constitution—or we shall have chaos. We cannot
> possibly imagine a successful form of government in
> which every individual citizen would have the right to

interpret the Constitution according to his own convictions, beliefs, and prejudices.[15]

When the two men met, Eisenhower did not suggest that Governor Faubus remove the troops. Rather, he encouraged him to change their orders. Faubus could direct the troops "to preserve order, but to allow the Negro children to attend Central High School."[16] Eisenhower also told Faubus that he did not want to see any governor humiliated. But if it came to a confrontation between federal and state governments, "the state would lose."[17]

Governor Faubus returned to Arkansas. But he did not remove the troops or change their orders.

The Governor Is Overruled

Thurgood Marshall, Daisy Bates, and the nine students went to court on Friday, September 20, for the hearing against the governor. Melba Pattillo hoped to meet Governor Faubus. She wanted him to see that there was "nothing so bad about [her] that he shouldn't allow white children to go to school with [her]."[18] But Governor Faubus did not show up at the hearing. His attorneys came alone. They made several motions to postpone the case. They even asked the judge to disqualify himself from presiding over the case. Judge Davies refused these motions and Faubus's attorneys left.

Thurgood Marshall was astounded. He had never seen anything like that in court. Judge Davies ordered that the hearing continue. He listened to Little Rock Mayor Woodrow Wilson Mann, school officials, Police

Chief Marvin Potts, and some of the nine students. They testified that there had not been significant threats to warrant the calling of the National Guard. Judge Davies ruled that Governor Faubus, by the use of the National Guard had, "thwarted" the court-approved plan for integration. He forbade the governor from further interference. Faubus had to remove the troops. The Little Rock Nine would start school on Monday.

The Mob Attacks

Judge Davies's decision was not welcome news to the growing crowd surrounding the school. By Monday, the mob raged and grew restless waiting for the African-American students to arrive. The National Guard was gone. A much smaller number of police was assigned to control the mob and protect the nine students.

The students met at Daisy Bates's home. They divided into two cars. For the students' safety, the drivers would take indirect routes to the school. Then the students would enter through a smaller side entrance in order to avoid the mob.

Reporters had also come to Daisy Bates's house to report the story. She asked the reporters not to follow the students for their safety. But she told four African-American reporters that if they were at the Sixteenth and Park Avenue entrance, they would see the Little Rock Nine enter the school.

The black reporters arrived at Sixteenth and Park streets before the students. As they got out of their car, the mob saw them and attacked. Shouts of "Get the niggers" echoed through the crowd. Two men lunged at the *Arkansas State Press*'s photographer, Earl Davy. They held him down and smashed his camera against the sidewalk. A burly man landed a blow to New York's *Amsterdam News* reporter Jimmy Hicks's shoulder. Hicks was spun around before he could run. He then hid between parked cars. Several other men hammered Alex Wilson, the editor of the *Tri-State Defender.* They knocked him to the ground and kicked his stomach. One hate-filled man raised a brick to smash Alex's skull. The reporters' lives were in grave danger. Then somebody yelled, "The niggers are in the school!"[19] The mob rushed toward the police barricades that surrounded Central High.

During the brutal attack on the reporters, the students hurried out of the cars and entered through the side door. They were led through the unfamiliar halls. They tried to ignore the ugly words as chants of "The niggers are in" grew louder.

Classes Begin

The students met with Vice Principal Elizabeth P. Huckaby and received their schedules. The stress had been hard on Thelma Mothershed's heart. Her pulse was irregular and she was having trouble breathing. She sank to the floor and rested her head on a chair. Her lips and fingers were bluish. Huckaby called the school nurse to care for her. The other students were guided to their classes. None of the nine had any classes together. They would each have to face the white students alone.

Some white students left school once the black students arrived. Others made unfriendly remarks, spat at them, or attempted to move their chairs away from the black students. Some teachers were against integration, too. They allowed abusive remarks in their classrooms. But not all of the students or teachers were unfriendly. Huckaby was pleased to see one of her better students helping Jefferson Thomas understand an assignment. And Melba's shorthand teacher had complete control of her classroom. She tried to steer Melba away from the scene growing outside the window.

Melba looked out anyway. The mob had grown. It was a sea of angry faces pushing against the barricades. Chants of "Two, Four, Six, Eight, We ain't gonna integrate" could be heard through the school's brick walls.

A Quick Exit

At around 11:30 A.M., Assistant Chief of Police Gene Smith realized his forces would not be able to hold the horde of people trying to get into the school. He ordered that the black students be removed from school for their own safety. Teachers ran to gather the nine students. Melba recalls the look of fear on her guide's face as she was told to hurry to the principal's office and not stop for anything.

Assistant Chief Smith was determined to get the kids out of the school unharmed. He directed them to the basement. Outside the basement, two sedans

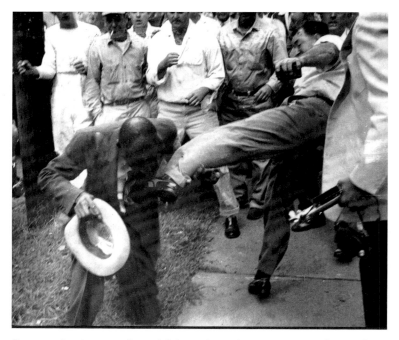

Segregationists watch as African-American reporter Alex Wilson is kicked in the chest outside Little Rock Central High School.

waited with their engines running. The students were told to get in, lock their doors, keep their heads down, and hold their notebooks against the windows. Then Smith told the drivers to move fast and not stop.

The drivers gunned the engines and surged through the crowd. They accelerated as the mass of people parted. Carlotta Walls peeked out of the window at one point: "If I was going to die, I wanted to see it coming."[20] The cars sped away from the school so fast that Carlotta feared they might run someone over.

Later, when everyone was safe, a reporter asked Daisy Bates if the students would return to Horace Mann, the all-black school. She said "No, they were going to remain out of the school until the president of the United States guaranteed them protection within Central High."[21]

Daisy Bates challenged President Eisenhower to rise to the occasion. But it was the mayor of Little Rock who sent an urgent telegram requesting help:

September 24, 1957, 10:37 A.M.

The immediate need for federal troops is urgent. The mob is much larger at 8 A.M. than at any time yesterday. People are converging on the scene from all directions. Mob is armed and engaging in fisticuffs and other acts of violence. Situation is out of control and police cannot disperse the mob. I am pleading to you as President of the United States, in the interest of humanity, law, and order, and because of democracy worldwide, to provide the necessary federal troops within several hours. Action by you will restore peace and order and compliance with your proclamation.

Woodrow Wilson Mann,
Mayor of Little Rock, Arkansas[22]

The Screaming Eagles Arrive

Midafternoon on September 24, President Dwight D. Eisenhower gave the order to send troops into Little Rock. That night, he addressed the nation from the

White House. He spoke of the "serious situation" in Arkansas:

> Disorderly mobs have deliberately prevented the carrying out of proper orders from a federal court . . . I yesterday issued a proclamation calling upon the mob to disperse. This morning the mob again gathered in front of the Central High School of Little Rock, obviously for the purpose of again preventing the carrying out of the Court's order relating to the admission of Negro children to that school. . . .
>
> I have today issued an executive order directing the use of troops under federal authority to aid in the execution of federal law at Little Rock, Arkansas. . . . Mob rule cannot be allowed to override the decisions of our courts.[23]

The secretary of defense called more than one thousand paratroopers into Little Rock. The soldiers came from the 101st Airborne Division. They were military heroes known as the "Screaming Eagles." Army planes delivered the battle-equipped men to the city. A parade of jeeps and army vehicles carried them to Central High.

It was after midnight when the nine students heard that they would start school the next day. This time, they would go in with military protection. At 8:25 A.M. on September 25, 1957, the Little Rock Nine gathered again at Daisy Bates's home. Around fifty soldiers were waiting. Their boots and rifles shined. Battle helmets

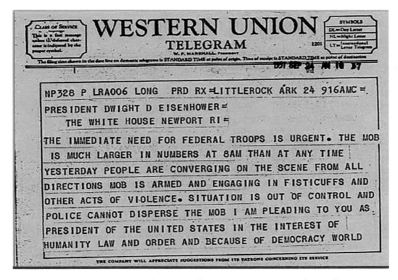

Little Rock Mayor Woodrow Wilson Mann wrote this telegram to President Eisenhower pleading for assistance from federal troops.

covered their heads. Some of the soldiers spoke into walkie-talkies. They told the Little Rock Nine that they would be riding to Central High in a jeep convoy.

Jeeps with gun mounts led and followed the army station wagon that held the students. A helicopter circled overhead. As they approached Central High, the students could see that the soldiers had blocked off streets around the school.

In the distance, the nine could still hear the chant "Two, Four, Six, Eight, We ain't gonna integrate." But the crowd was no longer a threat to the safety of the students or the school. The soldiers formed a box around the students and led them through the front doors.

Eisenhower's Stand on Race

President Eisenhower was moderate on civil rights. As a general, he initially opposed the desegregation of the Army. He also had many white friends and supporters in the South who were in favor of segregation. Sometimes he seemed uncomfortable with African-American leaders.

However, Eisenhower was generally against discrimination. In high school, he defended an African-American athlete who was harassed and kicked off a school team by the coach. Later, he refused to stay in a hotel because it said that African Americans and Jews were not welcome. As president, he continued the desegregation of the Army and even desegregated the Army schools before the Supreme Court's *Brown v. Board of Education* decision. He was also the first president to hire an African American for an executive position.

In a letter responding to famed African-American baseball player, Jackie Robinson, Eisenhower said that he was "firmly on record as believing that every citizen of every race and creed deserves to enjoy equal civil rights and liberties."[24]

But it was not the race issue that brought Eisenhower into the Little Rock conflict. Eisenhower saw danger in allowing a state to override a federal mandate.

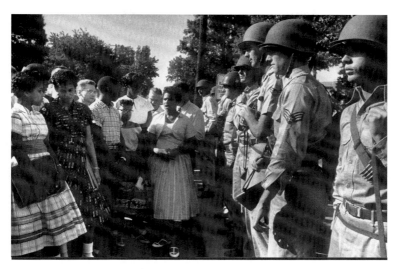

Minnijean Brown (center), along with six other black students, is blocked by the Arksansas National Guard from entering Central High School by order of Governor Faubus.

The nine students were both proud and sad. When Minnijean Brown first saw the soldiers, she told Daisy Bates, "For the first time in my life, I feel like an American citizen."[25] The others also were grateful that their country would go to such lengths so they could attend Central High. But as Ernest Green noted, "We got in, finally, because we were protected by paratroops." He was not sorry the president sent the troops. "[O]nly sorry it had to be that way."[26]

Even with the violence that occurred outside the school, the nine believed that the white students would like them if only they would get to know them. But most of the white students did not take the chance to find out.

Stormy Days at Central High

"It was like going into battle every day."[1]

—Ernest Green

Once the chaos of the early days had died down, the Little Rock Nine had to establish themselves as students at the school. They faced many challenges in their day-to-day activities. While most of the students did not blatantly oppose their presence in the school, there were also very few who openly accepted the nine black students.

Publicly, the school stated support for the newcomers and condemned the first days' violence. Student editors wrote in the school newspaper, *The Tiger*:

> No matter what our personal opinions may be, we cannot be proud of the violence that occurred around our school that made it necessary for the use of these Federal troops. Looking back on this year will probably be with regret that integration could not have been

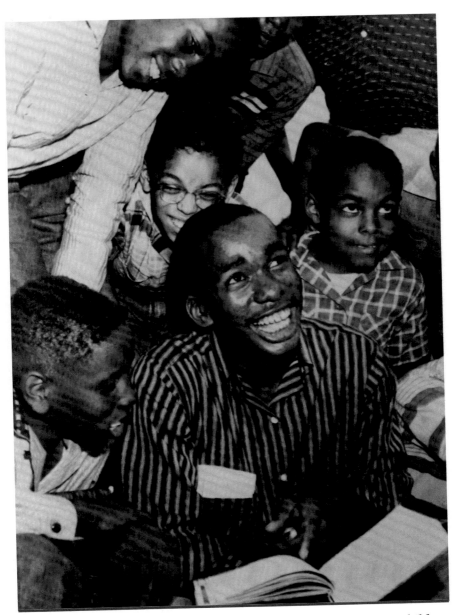

Ernest Green shows his textbooks to young African-American children after his first full day at Little Rock Central High School.

accomplished peacefully, without incident, without publicity.[2]

An earlier student editorial had encouraged students to "meet the challenge" with maturity and intelligence. And another reminded students that less than one percent of the Little Rock population was in the crowd on September 23.[3]

In general, students were concerned with their own affairs. Girls wore poodle skirts and bobby socks. The boys had crew cuts. They worried about their grades, after-school activities, and sports. They listened to music by Pat Boone, Elvis Presley, and Buddy Holly. They thought about things like the prom and dating. Most students chose to ignore the new African-American students.

But a group of segregationist students used every chance they had to make the nine African-American students' year a nightmare. These students yelled insults and threats, passed out mean-spirited flyers, spat on the black students, and even physically attacked them. The nine students were often shoved, kicked, or tripped as they tried to attend classes.

White students who initially were friendly to these new students also received threats. Others, who may have wanted to become friends, were scared off by these actions.

The Attacks Continue

The 101st Division had removed the crowd outside with efficiency and training. But inside the school

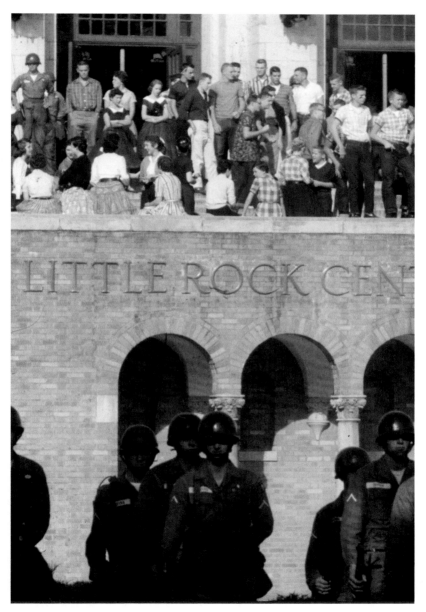

The 101st Airborne Division of the US Army stand guard at Central
High School in 1957.

they were told to stay in the background. Images of the armed guards entering Central High shocked the nation. False rumors that soldiers followed girls into the bathrooms spread and caused an uproar. School administrators wanting to regain control of their school asked the guardsmen not to interfere. Furthermore, the soldiers were told not to enter classrooms, locker rooms, bathrooms, or assemblies. The school did not want the guardsmen to be a disruption.

The African-American students were often left to fend off their attackers themselves. Carlotta described the atmosphere in the school hallways as "volatile." For her, it was a group of boys in leather jackets who were the worst offenders, spitting at her whenever they had the chance. She describes the first time it happened: "…without warning I felt something wet hit my face. I flinched. Immediately, I knew what it was. But who had done it? It was useless trying to single out the villain in the sea of smirking faces quickly moving past me."[4]

Other attacks were more serious. In the locker room, a combination lock struck Terrence's temple and knocked him to his knees. He stopped himself from falling by clinging to the locker's handle. If he fell, he was sure the attack would get worse. He stumbled into the coach's office. When he returned, the clothes in his locker were soaking wet. While he was with the coach, the boys had drenched his clothes.

In another instance, Melba was walking down a hallway when a boy flashed a shiny object in her face. Suddenly there was intense pain and burning in her eyes. "I thought I'd die," she remembers. "I couldn't hear or see or feel anything except that throbbing searing fire centered in my eyes."[5] Some type of acid or alkaline had been sprayed on her. Droplets immediately faded her blouse. The soldier assigned to protect Melba helped flush out her eyes with water.

Elizabeth went into Vice Principal Huckaby's office during the second week of school. She had been crying. "I want to go home," she told Huckaby.[6] She was tired of the name-calling and being hit by objects thrown at her. She was sick of getting tripped and kicked; it was all too much. She did not even know her attackers.

Huckaby talked her out of leaving. She felt that if the black students backed down, the attacks would get worse and it would be harder for them to return. She also worried that it would make it more difficult for other black students to integrate. She appealed to Elizabeth's courage. Reluctantly, Elizabeth agreed to stay.

From Bad to Worse

President Eisenhower's use of the Screaming Eagles to protect the black students was politically unpopular. Consequently, the president wanted to remove the troops from Central High School as quickly as possible. But the situation never became safe enough for him to remove the troops fully. So in November, the 101st Division soldiers were replaced by members of the National Guard under federal orders. Some of these men were the same ones who had blocked the nine students' entrance in September. These men were not as well trained as the 101st Division and there were fewer of them. Attacks on the nine students increased as their protection lessened.

Students regularly knocked the books out of Jefferson Thomas's arms. They kicked him as he bent to retrieve the books or sent his books flying down the halls. Once while he was standing at his locker, a boy landed such a brutal blow that Jefferson was knocked unconscious. His mother tried to keep him home the next day. But he told her, "No, if I stay out today, it'll be worse tomorrow."[7]

For all of the nine students, simply surviving at Central High was a daily battle. But as bad as it was, they did not always report the attacks to the teachers or principal. Reports not witnessed by a teacher would not be punished. Vice Principal Huckaby knew this was unfair. She also knew who the likely attackers were. But she believed suspending students based on unwitnessed accusations would cause more problems. It could give segregationists a way of removing the black students simply by lying. Huckaby felt that if white students were removed from school based on unwitnessed accusations from the black students, she would also have to remove the black students if the white students accused them of violent actions.[8]

A Peaceful Response

As the racial attacks continued, the nine students developed ways of handling some of the cutting remarks. They were inspired by civil rights leader Martin Luther King, Jr.'s actions. They read books by

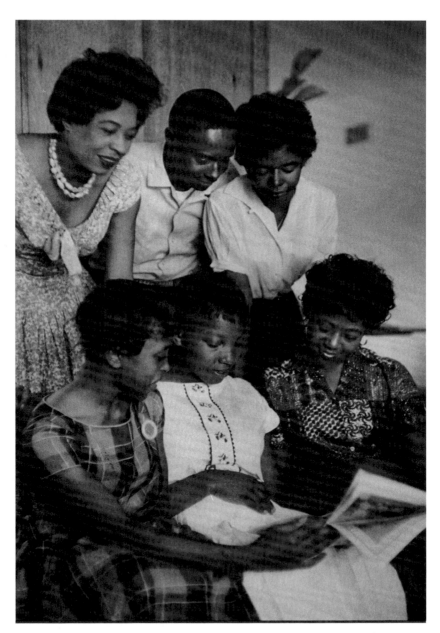

Daisy Bates, top left, spends time with the Little Rock students.

Mahatma Gandhi, who inspired King. Gandhi used nonviolent means to free India from British rule. King applied these nonviolent methods to the civil rights cause.

The nine students tried to follow the peaceful examples of these men. Melba said "thank you" to her attackers to show they could not get to her. Terrence invited boys who insulted his mother over to his house to meet her. As a group, the nine African-American students were determined not to give up. They leaned on each other as they tried to make it through the day.

The nine students received letters of support from people across the nation and around the world. Newspapers printed stories condemning the actions of Governor Faubus, the crowd outside the school, and others who were against integration. Several newspapers around the country ran a series of articles about the students such as "The Nine Who Dared."

Will Counts had photographed Elizabeth Eckford as she walked through the angry crowd the first day of school. His images gave the crisis a face—the face of a young dignified woman tormented simply because she was black. The picture was shown in newspapers across the country and made her a hero to many people outside her hometown.

One day, a white stranger knocked on Elizabeth's door. He was carrying a watch and handed it to Elizabeth. It was from his wife. She was dying of cancer and wanted Elizabeth to have it.[9] Knowing they were valued elsewhere helped the Little Rock Nine make it through the year.

Role Models for Nonviolence

In the 1940s, Mohandas (Mahatma) Gandhi encouraged the Indian people to stand up to unfair laws but never to become violent. Although thousands of Indians were arrested, they continued to protest the laws of the British government that controlled India. Gandhi's movement received sympathy from around the world. The British did not know how to combat this nonviolent approach. Eventually, India gained independence from Britain.

In his essay "Civil Disobedience," Henry David Thoreau promoted nonviolent resistance as a way of protesting unfair treatment. This essay, along with Gandhi's example, later influenced Martin Luther King Jr. King encouraged the use of peaceful resistance in protests throughout the country. He and many others, black and white Americans, were arrested for their civil disobedience as they peacefully broke unjust laws and accepted the punishment.

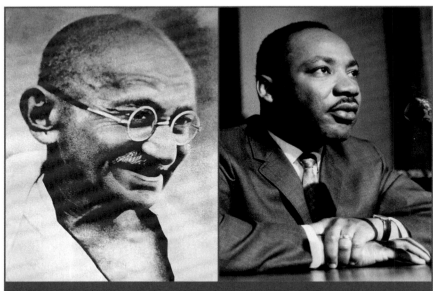

Ghandi and Martin Luther King Jr. inspired others to protest injustice in a peaceful manner.

Trouble for Minnijean

The nine students came to Central High for its opportunities. Central High was five stories tall. It had well-equipped science labs; a greenhouse; rooms and machines for vocational interests such as wood-working, plumbing, and drafting; and a library with eleven thousand books. It offered excellent college preparatory classes. Students put on fully-costumed plays in a two thousand-seat auditorium.

The nine students had been active in their old school. They were serious about their studies and enjoyed their extracurricular activities. Jefferson Thomas was a track star. Ernest Green played the saxophone. Melba Pattillo and Minnijean Brown loved to sing. But the black students had to give up their after-school activities if they wanted to attend Central High.

During his initial interviews with the black students, Superintendent Blossom told them that they would not be allowed to attend football or basketball games, participate in choir or drama club, or be on the track team. They could not go to prom or participate in other social events.[10] It was one of the ways the school board had reduced the number of students who wanted to integrate. It also was a way to maintain separation among the races. Segregationist parents worried that open social situations might lead to the black and white students dating—something that they were strongly against.

It was hard for the Little Rock Nine to give up the after-school activities they had enjoyed. But it seemed especially difficult for Minnijean. Minnijean had a fine voice and wanted to show the students at Central High that she had talent. She thought her ability to sing might help others accept her. She desperately wanted to fit in. Minnijean asked Vice Principal Huckaby if she could audition for the Christmas talent show. She had already been denied permission to sing at an earlier event. Huckaby said that the audition date had passed. Minnijean was heartbroken.

Minnijean's mother and Daisy Bates went to the school to discuss the situation. More importantly, they also wanted to discuss the lack of control the school had over the aggressive students. They talked about an episode in which Minnijean was kicked and nothing had been done about it. The principal said they had investigated, but since there were no witnesses, they were unable to verify the charge.[11]

Inaccurate reports about this meeting leaked to the press. The *Arkansas Democrat* printed that Bates and Mrs. Brown had come to Central High to protest Minnijean's not being in the talent show. This exposure made Minnijean more of a target for the segregationist students. Her expressive and reactive nature added fuel to the fiery situation. White students harassed Minnijean even more.

Just before winter break, the pressure got to Minnijean. It was lunch time. Minnijean had just filled her bowl with chili and was headed back to her table. Two boys pushed out their chairs to stop her from getting through. She was trapped. Other students kicked at her. The boys pulled their chairs back in. But as Minnijean started forward, they pushed them out again. This was not the first time things like this had happened in the lunchroom.

The cafeteria quieted as students noticed the conflict. Minnijean stood there, holding her tray above her head. She tried to get through, but could not. She wavered for a moment. Then she let go of the tray. As it crashed to the floor, hot, greasy chili splashed onto her tormentors.

Some of the black food servers clapped for Minnijean. They were tired of seeing the black students picked on. A teacher quickly escorted Minnijean and the two boys to the principal's office.

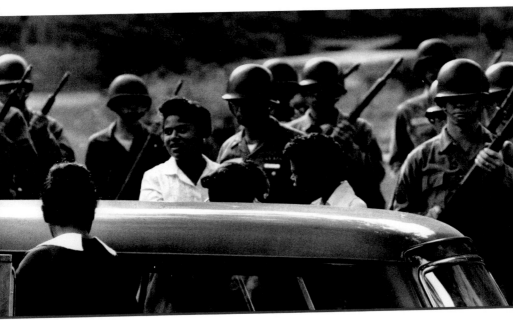

Minnijean Brown is seen here arriving at Central High in 1957. Her strong personality made it difficult for her to quietly endure all of the harassment that occurred at school.

The boys claimed that moving their chairs had been an accident, but they also defended Minnijean. She was so often teased that they did not blame her for getting mad. They even suggested that she may have dropped the tray accidentally. The boys were told to go home and change. Minnijean was suspended for six days.

The principal warned Minnijean that another episode like the one in the lunchroom would lead to expulsion. To return, she would have to agree not to retaliate verbally or physically to any harassment.

The attacks against Minnijean increased when she came back. Her attackers wanted her to react. They wanted her expelled. Once she was kicked so hard that she could not sit for two days.

On February 6, a girl following Minnijean kept stepping on her heels while chanting the word "nigger." As they neared the classroom, Minnijean had had enough. She swung around and called the girl "white trash." The white girl threw her purse at Minnijean and both girls were sent to the principal's office. The white girl went home, but Minnijean stayed at school. The principal thought it was best to wait before deciding on a punishment for the quarrel.

Students blamed Minnijean for the white girl going home and taunted her in the halls. During lunch, a boy poured hot soup down Minnijean's back. The boy routinely caused trouble and often harassed the African-American students. In the office, Vice Principal Huckaby asked him why he poured the soup on Minnijean. He said that he remembered "she had poured soup on some white boys and [so he] went over and dumped some on her."[12] The boy was suspended and Minnijean went home.

Shortly after, Minnijean learned she was expelled. The expulsion notice restated her agreement to not retaliate. Then it explained the reason she had been expelled: "After provocation of a girl student, [Minnijean] called the girl 'white trash,' after which the girl threw her purse at Minnijean."[13]

The real reason she was expelled had little to do with her name-calling. School administrators could not

Minnijean Brown (right) arrives with her mother, Imogene, at LaGuardia Airport in New York City after being expelled from Little Rock Central High School.

combat the growing hostility focused on Minnijean. She was a target, and it was easier to remove her than to deal with the aggressors. Huckaby was worried about Minnijean's safety and the safety of the other eight students if Minnijean remained at Central High. Huckaby wrote in her memoir that the expulsion of Minnijean was "an admission of defeat" on the school's part. "It was not volatile, natural Minnijean that was our difficulty. It was just that she and our impossible situation would not mix."[14]

The segregationists saw Minnijean's expulsion as a win. They had found a way to remove an African-American student from Central High. Signs were printed and students chanted, "One down and eight to go."

The NAACP asked for a formal hearing to challenge Minnijean's expulsion. The school refused to discuss the matter. Minnijean would not be allowed back at Central High. The New Lincoln School in New York gave Minnijean a scholarship so that she could attend school there. Psychologist Kenneth Clark offered her a place to stay. Before she left Arkansas, she told a reporter, "They throw rocks, they spill ink on your clothes, they call you 'nigger,' they just keep bothering you every five minutes."[15] Minnijean would finish her schooling away from the torments at Central High.

Attacks and Threats Hit Home

Students at Central High were not the only ones causing trouble for the Little Rock Nine. Citizens against integration made life miserable for everyone involved in the desegregation process. They formed groups whose sole purpose was to stop integration. Two of these groups, the Capital Citizens' Council and the Mothers' League of Central High, held meetings, took out ads, and filed lawsuits all in an effort to end integration. Despite their claims of nonviolence, they encouraged the attacks that occurred during the first days of school at Central High.

In October, the Mothers' League decided to organize a walkout as a form of protest. At the designated time, the hall filled with a group of uncertain students. Teachers watched to see who would leave. Only about 150 students joined the protest. Half of those noticed the small numbers, walked out the front door, and came back in the side door. About seventy students who had left the building received suspensions.

Anonymous bomb threats were often called in to the school. These calls were usually hoaxes. But occasionally the threat was real. Once dynamite was found in the school basement. Another time, firecrackers were found in a student's locker.[1] Real or not, these calls disrupted the school day and forced unplanned evacuations and costly searches.

Many of the threats targeted Daisy Bates and the nine students' homes and families. The school directory published all students' addresses and phone numbers, including those of the Little Rock Nine. This made it easy for segregationists to find out where the

Burning crosses was one way for segregationists to try to intimidate those who supported integration.

nine students lived. The students received hate mail. Their phones rang at all hours with abusive calls. Bomb threats were common. Once, someone called Terrence's mother to say her son had been seriously injured. She rushed to the school only to learn it was a prank.[2]

During the first year of integration, crosses were burned in the front yard of the Bates's home three times. The front-room picture windows were shattered so many times, that Daisy and L.C. covered them with steel screens. Vandals set their house on fire twice. Their insurance company dropped their policy because of the number of claims. And the Bateses had to hire private guards to protect their home.

Bates Fights Back

In October, the Little Rock city council passed a law requiring organizations to give information about their members to any elected official who asked for them. The city council wanted to know who was supporting the NAACP. Daisy Bates refused to hand over the documents. She knew that giving the information would lead to harassment of NAACP members and donors.

Two weeks later, the city council ordered the arrests of NAACP officials because they refused to cooperate. Daisy Bates turned herself in to the police. The judge in Little Rock said the ordinance was valid. He fined Bates one hundred dollars plus legal costs. The NAACP appealed. The case went all the way to the US Supreme Court. The Supreme Court declared the law unconstitutional and Bates did not have to pay the fine.

A Tough Blow

Daisy Bates knew from the beginning that she was risking a lot by helping the black students integrate. Early in the fall, a white woman came to Bates and asked her to convince the black students not to attend Central High. Bates asked what would happen if she refused. The woman told her that her paper would fail. "You'll be destroyed," she said. "You, your newspaper, your reputation—everything."[3]

Daisy Bates did not back down. She would not abandon the nine students. During the crisis, advertisers pulled their ads from her newspaper. One longtime advertiser told Bates that he had been threatened. Someone had said his store would be bombed if he continued to support the *Arkansas State Press*. He was sorry, but he did not feel he could take the risk.

The Bateses tried to keep the paper running for as long as they could. Many letters of encouragement came into their office. A few letters contained cash gifts to help keep the paper going. But since papers do not charge a lot of money for each issue, they cannot survive without advertisers. Ultimately the segregationists won that battle. The *Arkansas State Press* went out of business.

Jobs in Jeopardy

Some of the parents lost their jobs because they sent their children to the formerly all-white school. Threats

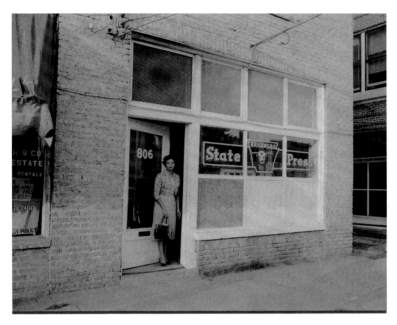

Daisy Bates stands in the doorway of the *Arkansas State Press* newspaper in 1957.

to job security were some of the hardest to cope with. Without a paycheck, parents could not afford to feed their families.

The school where Melba's mother taught refused to renew her teaching contract unless she withdrew Melba from Central High. Melba recalls the food cupboards getting bare as her mother dealt with their financial crisis.[4] Melba's mother contacted the newspaper and the bishops in the area. With their help, she convinced the school to continue her employment in the fall.

Graduation Time

"It seemed as though all of Little Rock—maybe even the entire nation—was holding its breath. This was the most publicized commencement in history, and all of the attention boiled down to this moment."[1]

—Carlotta Walls LaNier

As the end of the year approached, the attacks on the black students got worse. Their lockers were often broken into and their books and other items stolen. Threatening phone calls to the homes of the students became more frequent. Melba received a call from someone who told her, "We're offering ten thousand dollars for your head on a platter."[2]

Amid the turmoil, some students and teachers tried to help the African-American students. A boy named Link went to the segregationist meetings. Afterward, he called Melba and told her what they planned and places she should avoid.

Several teachers kept watch in the hallway between classes to help deter attacks. Gloria Ray was walking down the stairs when she heard a teacher scream out a warning. A boy was coming up from behind to push Gloria down the stairs. Gloria grabbed the railing and hurried down before the boy reached her. The teacher's warning saved Gloria from serious injury.

Last-Minute Worries

The end of the year brought new concerns to Ernest Green's mind. He was the only senior in the group. The segregationists were looking for any reason they could find to exclude him from the graduation ceremony. Rumors were spreading that he would not be allowed to walk with the other Central High graduates. One student told Melba that for the African-American students it was not going to be a graduation; it would be a funeral.[3]

Ernest was under a lot of pressure. He wondered if they could stop him from graduating with his class. He wanted reassurance that he would be protected if he did. Daisy Bates met with Congressman Hays and visited the secretary of the Army at the Pentagon in Washington, DC. Bates came back and told Ernest that there would be protection at the graduation.

There was also some concern about Ernest's grades. The physics teacher believed in segregation. He had not allowed Ernest to make up the work from the first three weeks of school when the African-American teens were barred from entering. Most of Ernest's grades were fine, but he needed to pass physics.

Ernest Green proudly shows his diploma to his family.

Ernest received a letter from an anonymous source. The letter asked that he not attend the graduation so that the white students could graduate without any trouble. Although the letter was signed "a worried senior," it was clearly written by an adult.

Ernest stayed home on the day of the senior picnic. But he did not intend to stay home for his graduation. He had gone through too much. He felt that graduating from Central [High] was bigger than just him. He figured if "one of us graduated, people could never refer to Central High as an all-white school again."[4]

Planning the Event

The school began planning for the ceremony. Traditionally, students were called alphabetically—boy, girl, boy, girl. After receiving their diplomas, the boy and girl would walk down the steps together. This was a problem. Although Ernest had never shown interest in any of the girls at Central High, the idea of a black and white couple was shocking in many places in America. In many states, it was illegal for a black person and a white person to marry. In some places, even the suggestion of a black man being involved with a white woman could lead to his murder.

The principal thought it would be best to let the girls know that they did not have to walk down the steps with Ernest. They could wait and leave a slight gap. Vice Principal Huckaby was uncertain exactly which girl would walk with Ernest. But she talked to the five girls whose names were near his alphabetically. One graduating senior, Ann Emerson, immediately said that she would have no problems walking with Ernest if her name was called.[5]

There were two graduation events at Central High. The first was an optional religious ceremony. It was scheduled the Sunday before graduation and took place in Central High's giant football stadium. The actual graduation was Tuesday. On that day, Ernest would receive his diploma. For both ceremonies, police and members of the National Guard would offer protection.

On Sunday, Ernest's parents arrived at the stadium early. At first, people seemed to be avoiding the seats around Mr. and Mrs. Green. But soon others arrived and sought out those seats as a sign of support. There were no incidents during the hour-long service. But afterward, off to the side, a senior boy spat on a young

African-American girl who had been attending. Police arrested the boy.

On Monday, the seniors practiced for graduation. Before practice began, the class president, Ronnie Hubbard, spoke to the other seniors. "I know everyone will do what is right tomorrow night," he told them. "I don't think anyone wants to do anything to ruin our commencement." The seniors applauded, and practice went smoothly.[6]

A Distinguished Guest

Tuesday was graduation day, and tension permeated everything. Final exams had been graded and turned in. Ernest had passed all his classes and would walk on stage to receive his diploma. Captain Stumbaugh of the FBI assured Vice Principal Huckaby that the safety preparations were complete. He had even checked the upper windows of the houses overlooking the stadium for possible sniper positions.

In the stadium, the police presence was noticeable. The principal gave each senior only three tickets for family and friends. By doing this, he hoped to keep down the number of troublemakers.

At 8:00 P.M., six hundred seniors in their caps and gowns proceeded into the stadium and found their seats. The program consisted of speeches and a long epic poem. There was no mention of the desegregation crisis.

Finally, the gym teacher began announcing the names of the graduating class. Ernest was Number 203. His name was called. He walked up the ramp and

Ernest Green was the first black student to graduate from Little Rock Central High School.

onto the stage. The principal handed him his diploma and then shook his hand. The few photographers admitted to the ceremony tried to get the best pictures they could to send over the newswire. Ernest had made it. He was the first African American to graduate from Central High.

On his way back from receiving his degree, Ernest was alone. The girl who had walked with Ernest at the religious service received so many negative phone calls that a teacher decided it was best if she left some space between them.

Dr. Martin Luther King Jr. (center) talks with Ernest Green and Daisy Bates at Ernest's graduation from Central High.

Watching Ernest receive his diploma and sitting with his parents was civil rights leader Dr. Martin Luther King Jr. King had been speaking nearby in Pine Bluff, Arkansas, and decided to come see Ernest graduate. It did not matter what the rest of the crowd felt or that a few people had whistled while Ernest was on stage. He had graduated, and Martin Luther King Jr., a hero in the civil rights movement, was there to see.

The Year the Schools Closed

Many people in Little Rock breathed a sigh of relief once the school year came to a close. They hoped that the worst of the crisis had passed. Unfortunately, this was wishful thinking. The battle was far from over.

Barely a month after Ernest Green graduated from Central High, the school board asked the court for permission to stop integration until 1961. They pointed to the chaos of the previous school year, arguing that desegregation had been too great of a distraction. Judge Lemley heard the case and granted the three-year delay. He said that while black students had the right to attend white schools, "the time ha[d] not come for them to enjoy [that right.]"[1] Melba worried that her year of torture had been for nothing.

The NAACP was outraged. They appealed to the US Circuit Court of Appeals in St. Louis. The appeals court overturned the decision in August, but left time for the case to be heard by the US Supreme Court.

The LITTLE ROCK NINE and SCHOOL DESEGREGATION

When Governor Faubus learned the delay was overturned, he called a special session of the legislature. A governor may call a special session to consider bills after the regular legislative session has finished. The bill that Governor Faubus wanted passed would give him the power to close all public schools to avoid integration. The state representatives voted overwhelmingly to pass the bill.

On September 12, 1958, three announcements were made that directly affected the African-American students at Central High. First, the Supreme Court ordered Little Rock to continue its planned integration. Within hours, the Little Rock school board announced that schools would begin in three days. These were the decisions the African-American students were hoping for.

Then on the very same day as those other two announcements, Governor Faubus used his new power and closed all the public high schools in Little Rock: Central High School; Hall High School, a segregated white school; and Horace Mann, the segregated black school, were closed by order of the governor. The citizens would vote in two weeks to decide if these schools should remain closed.

The WEC Is Formed

The citizens would vote in only a few weeks. One of the most respected senior citizens in Little Rock, Adolphine Fletcher Terry, organized a group of women to fight against the school closings. She called the

Thurgood Marshal stands outside the Supreme Court in Washington, DC.

Who Was Orval Faubus?

It is surprising that an integration crisis happened in Little Rock, Arkansas. Little Rock was considered progressive before 1957, and Governor Orval Faubus initially seemed moderate on racial issues.

Faubus grew up in rural Arkansas. The son of a socialist, Faubus ran for office as a champion of the poor. Before the

Governor Orval Faubus

crisis, Faubus avoided taking sides on racial issues. He campaigned against an extreme segregationist and won. He appointed African Americans to state offices. After his election, two Arkansas school districts integrated without any major problems.

In 1957 Faubus faced a political crisis. A large number of voters were against integration. In order to be reelected, Faubus would have to side with the segregationists. His political ambition was stronger than any beliefs he held on racial equality. Calling out the troops to protect the nine African-American children would have placed him on the same side as the integrationists.

Faubus won four more elections after the crisis. He was the longest-serving governor in the state. But his name is forever tied to the crisis he helped create in Little Rock and the closing of the schools.

group the Women's Emergency Committee to Open Our Schools, or WEC for short.

WEC immediately began educating the public and working to get out the vote. But the vote did not come out in their favor. At the end of September, 19,470 people voted "against racial integration of all schools within the school district." Only 7,561 voted "for racial integration."[2] WEC was unhappy with the way the ballot was worded. The ballot did not ask about closing the schools. Instead it asked if the voter was for or against integration. The schools remained closed, but WEC did not give up.

Scrambling for a School

Students in tenth through twelfth grade hurried to find new schools. Some students were sent to live with relatives out of state. These students left their friends and families behind. It was hard, but in time most made new friends and found new opportunities.

Other students took long bus rides to schools outside the city. The additional students overcrowded the classrooms. Goforth Coleman hitchhiked almost twenty miles to school each way. "[T]he classes were so full—they had about 40 students per class," he recalled. "It was not a very conducive place for learning, yet the teachers worked real hard with us."[3]

Private schools opened for white students. At first, the school district tried to lease the closed schools to the Little Rock Private School Corporation. The school district wanted to use public money to fund these segregated private schools. Judges at the Eighth

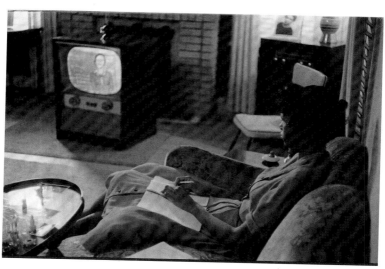

An unidentified African-American girl uses a television lesson to study at home after the schools were closed in Little Rock in 1958.

Circuit Court of Appeals stopped this action. They said that the Supreme Court decision was the "law of the land" and the court would not allow "evasive schemes for segregation."[4]

Some schools opened inside churches. These schools had little time to hire teachers and plan for classes. Mary Peterson was starting tenth grade the year the schools were closed. Instead of attending Central High, she went to the school sponsored by the Second Baptist Church. The curriculum was basic, but she enjoyed eating lunch at a nearby drugstore. She remembers an older teacher holding class on her porch when the teacher's arthritis acted up and another teacher sending students to her house to pick up things she had forgotten.

"Those were 'trustier' times," said Mary. She continued:

> I don't want to give the impression that the whole year was wasted. There were very good teachers there. . . . I remember capable teachers for world history and biology. I think part of the problem was having to hire people in a hurry and get a school up and running from the get go.[5]

The seven remaining African-American students were caught in the middle of this political tug of war. Melba remembers waiting. "I waited for legislators and Faubus and the NAACP to resolve the entanglement that surrounded Central High's integration. . . . I was alone, at home, waiting to restart my life—waiting to live my teenage years."[6]

For some students, the year was lost forever. As many as 45 percent of black seniors and 15 percent of white seniors in Little Rock did not continue their education that year.[7] Many of these students found jobs but did not graduate.

Although school was closed, extracurricular activities continued. There were dances, a school newspaper, and regular football games. But they were a poor substitute for school. Many football players were forced to decide which was more important: playing the game or getting an education by going to school out of the district. Football players lost their eligibility to play if they went to school outside the area.

Students stand in front of Central High School after it was closed
by Governor Faubus and the residents of Little Rock.

When the season ended, the football players just
left. Central High's team never even had a group
photo taken. The other activities dwindled as parents
realized the schools would remain closed.

Saving the Teachers

The high school teachers' contract required them to be
in the classroom from 8:30 A.M. until 3:30 P.M. every
day. The teachers came, but there were no students.
It was frustrating not to have students to teach. They
began to teach each other. At Horace Mann, Principal
Leroy M. Cristophe brought in lecturers from local
colleges to teach his faculty. "Dr. Cristophe certainly
kept us busy," remembered Jerome Muldrew, a young
teacher at the time.[8]

The teachers were not allowed to teach outside of the schools until after 3:30 P.M. But many were committed to the education of children and would begin tutoring at 3:31 P.M.

In December 1958, the citizens elected a new Little Rock school board. The new board members were evenly split on the segregation issue. In May, the three board members who supported integration walked out of a meeting in protest. They were angry at what segregationists were proposing. They believed that the meeting would end after they left because there would no longer be a quorum. A quorum is the minimum number of people needed for voting to be allowed.

But the remaining members continued the meeting. Since a quorum was present when the meeting started, the decisions were still valid. The remaining board members fired forty-four teachers and school administrators who they believed favored integration. This included Vice Principal Huckaby, who the nine African-American students had turned to for help.

Huckaby and most of these teachers were beloved members of the community. They were fired because they had followed the law and tried to treat African-American children fairly. In response to these dismissals, city businessmen formed an organization called Stop This Outrageous Purge (STOP). They wanted the teachers rehired.

STOP joined WEC in an effort to recall the election of the school board members. They succeeded in forcing a new election. The vote was close. But the segregationists were voted out while the three moderate board members kept their positions. The new school board rehired thirty-nine of the forty-four teachers who had lost their jobs.

Back to School at Last

The school closings lasted an entire academic year. Then in June 1959, the US district court found the school-closing law unconstitutional. The school board chose not to appeal the decision.

Carlotta and Jefferson registered for Central High. They were the only members of the original nine still in high school. The NAACP had asked families to sponsor and give the remaining students places to live while they continued their education. Melba went to live with a family in Santa Anna, California. Terrence moved to Los Angeles. Thelma Mothershed took correspondence courses and earned enough credits to graduate.

With less than two weeks' notice, the school board announced that classes would start a month early on August 12. This surprise act limited the amount of time segregationists had to plan.

Even with late notice, around 250 protesters arrived at Central High on the first day of school. This time the police were ready and in control. They turned fire hoses on the members of the crowd who tried to break through the police lines. They arrested twenty-one people and the crowd scattered.

There were a few more incidents that year. Two women threw tear gas into the school during a school

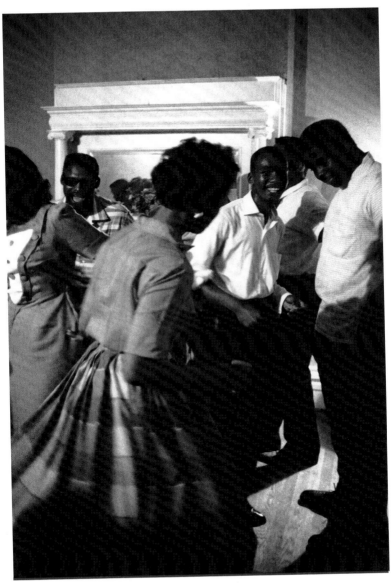

Students dance at a graduation party for the Little Rock Nine in May 1958. Among them is Ernest Green (second from right, with rolled up sleeves).

board meeting. There were no injuries. A dynamite blast wrecked an empty office at the school administration building. The planner of that attack had strong ties to the Capital Citizens' Council.

At the end of the school year, Jefferson and Carlotta joined Ernest as the first African Americans to graduate from Central High School. While the Little Rock schools would not be fully integrated until 1972, the crisis was over.

Progress and Promise

"We have to act. All of us have to act. Each of us has to do. Especially our young people must seek out people who are different from themselves and speak freely and frankly to discover they share the same dreams.[1]

—President Bill Clinton

It has been more than fifty years since the Little Rock Nine stepped into Central High School for the first time. For those nine African Americans, and for the country, much has changed.

In 1997, the Little Rock Nine returned to Central High. They were there to commemorate the fortieth anniversary of the 1957 desegregation. The school itself looked the same. But instead of crowds heckling or jeering, they were applauding. The doors to the school were opened to the nine former students by President Bill Clinton and the governor of Arkansas, Mike Huckabee.

Those who gathered came to mark the time as well as to forgive and be forgiven. They were there to both appreciate the progress that had been made and continue the work for a more unified country. President Clinton addressed the crowd:

> On September 4th, 1957, Elizabeth Eckford walked to this door for her first day of school, utterly alone. She was turned away by people who were afraid of change, instructed by ignorance, hating what they simply could not understand. And America saw her, haunted and taunted for the simple color of her skin, and in the image we caught a very disturbing glimpse of ourselves.
>
> We saw not one nation under God, indivisible, with liberty and justice for all, but two Americas, divided and unequal. . . .
>
> Forty years later, we know that we all benefit—all of us—when we learn together, work together, and come together. That is, after all, what it means to be an American.[2]

Over the years, the nine former students have come back to Little Rock for various occasions. The first time they all returned to Central High School was for the thirtieth anniversary of the crisis. When asked by a reporter what they were feeling, Melba Pattillo replied, ""We are joyous that we made it, sad that we had to make it."[3] That night, they talked as old friends with both laughter and tears as they remembered together.

Elizabeth Eckford poses for a portrait in front of the main entrance of Central High School on September 13, 2007.

Only one of the nine came back to live in Little Rock as a young person. Elizabeth Eckford returned to Arkansas at age thirty. She came back because she wanted to be near her family. She freely admits having posttraumatic stress disorder from her year at Central High, but she refuses to hate people. She was angry, but she has chosen to forgive.

Healing Old Wounds

In 1957, photographer Will Counts photographed Elizabeth Eckford walking in front of a hateful crowd.

Her white and black skirt was starched and crisp. Dark sunglasses covered her eyes. Behind her was another young face. This girl's face was twisted with hatred and anger. The young white girl was Hazel Bryan. She was in the crowd yelling insults at Elizabeth. It is a photo that Elizabeth does not particularly like looking at.

The image was nominated for a Pulitzer Prize for photojournalism. The Pulitzer Prize is one of the highest American awards a person can win. The photo became a symbol of the civil rights movement. But pictures capture only a moment in time. Had things changed?

Forty years later, Will Counts was back in Arkansas covering the anniversary. He talked to Elizabeth Eckford and Hazel Bryan, now Hazel Massery, and asked if they would have their picture taken together forty years later.

In 1962, Massery had called and apologized to Eckford and to Eckford's grandmother. Hazel was only fifteen when the photo was taken. She was raised in a racist society and never questioned whether it was right or wrong. Massery says the birth of her first child opened her eyes. She became keenly aware of the pain she caused someone else's child. She looked at her heritage of hate and racism and decided not to pass it on to her children.[4]

"I was an immature 15-year-old," she said. "That's the way things were. I grew up in segregated society and I thought that was the way it was and that's the way it should be." Now she says she wants "to be the

In this photo by Will Counts, Hazel Bryan (now Hazel Massery) screams slurs at Elizabeth Eckford as she tries to attend Central High School on September 4, 1957.

link between the past and the future. I don't want to pass this along to another generation."[5]

Both Eckford and Massery agreed to meet and be photographed. The two women talked as Will set up the photo shoot. The two mothers were older and more mature. As they talked, they found they had a lot in common. They decided to have lunch. Then they enrolled in a class on race relations together. The second photo ran on the front page of the *Arkansas Democrat-Gazette*. It was a symbol of healing and an acknowledgement of how far Americans have come.

Honoring the Nine

After the black students' first year at Central High, the NAACP awarded Daisy Bates and the Little Rock Nine the Spingarn Medal. The Spingarn Medal is awarded annually for outstanding achievement by an African American. In 1999, the United States Congress awarded the United States Congressional Gold Medal to the Little Rock Nine. This is the highest honor the United States can give a civilian for service to the country. To many people the Little Rock Nine are heroes.

But they did not set out to be heroes. "We were not being courageous," explained Minnijean Brown, now Minnijean Brown Trickey. "We were kids who just wanted to go to school."[6] Elizabeth Eckford describes the nine as "ordinary people." But she reminds us all that "ordinary people can do extraordinary things."[7]

While the Little Rock Nine carry scars from their year at Central High, they would not change it. "I wouldn't take anything for our journey," said Ernest Green. "If one young person is inspired by the story, then the Little Rock Nine become the Little Rock 10, the 10 a hundred, the 10,000, the 10 million. . . ."[8]

The legacy of the desegregation of Central High School is much larger than the integration of a single school. The Little Rock crisis was a part of the American civil rights movement. The civil rights movement was the struggle of African Americans to gain the rights that were granted to all citizens by the Constitution. It was a chaotic time as people learned

Daisy Bates, in a wheelchair, carries the Olympic flame in Little Rock on May 26, 1996. She was one of many torch bearers for the Olympic Games, held in Atlanta, Georgia, that year.

to give up their prejudices and embrace the ideas of equality.

In many ways, the civil rights movement started with the NAACP's effort to desegregate the schools and the *Brown v. Board of Education* decision. Those actions led African Americans such as Rosa Parks to stand up for their rights. Sit-ins and rallies followed. Martin Luther King, Jr., led two hundred thousand supporters to Washington, DC. In 1964, all these efforts paid off. The United States Congress passed the Civil Rights Act and ended the Jim Crow laws.

The Civil Rights Act of 1964 grants equal access to public places such as restaurants, hotels, and movie theaters. And it entitles all people to the equal enjoyment of the goods, services, facilities, privileges, advantages, and accommodations of any place of public accommodation without discrimination by race, color, religion, gender, or national origin.

A Tribute to the Struggle

In 1998, Central High School was named a historic site because of its importance in the civil rights movement. A well-preserved 1950s-era gas station across the street became a museum and visitor center. Elizabeth Eckford's daughter often guides people around the building. She works for the National Park Service. Inside are televised and printed images from the 1957 crisis. The Little Rock crisis was covered in depth by the media. Americans and world citizens alike were witnesses to the events. Their opinions, both horrified and shocked,

Large crowds attend the fiftieth anniversary of the integration of Little Rock Central High School on September 25, 2007.

may have helped President Eisenhower decide to call in federal troops.

In August 2005, the Little Rock Nine gathered again to unveil a statue in their honor. The sculpture by John and Kathy Deering shows the nine on their courageous walk to Central High. It is placed outside the governor's office where Faubus called out the National Guard to stand in their way.

In May 2006, Thelma Mothershed-Wair and Elizabeth Eckford sank shovels into the dirt where a new visitor center would stand. The old visitor center was too small as the number of visitors continued to increase. The new building opened in September 2007 and is almost six times larger than the colorful little gas station. Much of the new center is devoted to telling the story of the 1957 desegregation. It houses materials related to the event and is a place where researchers can study those items. The new center also acts as a gateway for people who want to visit the historic neighborhood.

Perhaps the biggest tribute to what the Little Rock Nine achieved is the school itself. Central High School is fully integrated and educating students of all races together. "The bravery shown by these young people and their families changed the face of public education in this country," said Nancy Rousseau, principal of Central High School, talking about the Little Rock Nine. "Now, 2,400 students celebrate their differences every day, thanks to [their] courage."[9]

Closer to the Dream

Some of the Little Rock Nine speak at schools and colleges around the country. They do not want people to forget the importance of education and the dream of integration. But as President Clinton noted at the fortieth anniversary, while "segregation is no longer the law . . . too often, separation is still the rule."[10] The people of the United States are less racist, but the nation is still not fully integrated.

In small towns like Ferguson, Missouri, and big cities like New York, conflicts over race continue. In school cafeterias, students of different ethnic backgrounds tend to eat together. The public money spent on a student's education differs depending on where that student lives. Today's separation is not only by

The Road to Change

Central High School looks very much the same in 2015 as it did in 1957. But a great deal has changed over the years. The school is now located on Daisy L. Gatson Bates Drive, in honor of the woman who worked so passionately for integration. The student body is now more than 60% black.[11] Still, the school and the city continue to face challenges around race and integration.

At Central High, some students are honoring the Little Rock Nine with a memory project called "Mapping the Road to Change." The project is a publication that includes "essays written and selected by Central High students based on oral history interviews with older family & friends about personal experiences involving civil rights and human rights issues during their lifetimes."[12] The publication is a way for students to embrace their school's past and pass on lessons learned to future generations.

From left, Thelma Mothershed-Wair, Minnijean Brown Trickey, Jefferson Thomas, Terrence Roberts, Carlotta Wallls LaNier, Gloria Ray Karlmark, Ernest Green, Elizabeth Eckford, and Melba Pattillo Beals attend the fiftieth anniversary of the Central High integration.

race but also by economic situation or the amount of money a family has.

Standing outside Central High, President Clinton asked the young people to decide if they would be a "shining example or stunning rebuke to the world of tomorrow. . . . We are white and black, Asian and Hispanic, Christian and Jew and Muslim," President Clinton told the crowd. "But above all, we are still Americans. Martin Luther King said, 'We are woven into a seamless garment of destiny. We must be one America.'"[11]

We are closer than ever to achieving Martin Luther King Jr.'s dream of a unified country. The progress made over the past sixty years is a testament to all of the brave people of all races who have been willing to take a stand for equality. That progress needs to continue, with every new generation speaking out against injustice and inequality. The Little Rock Nine started out as nine black teenagers who just wanted to get a good education. They ended up inspiring the country and changing the face of American schools for the better.

Where Are They Now?

The Little Rock Nine proved their potential during the crisis they endured as teenagers. They all went on to receive college degrees and have successful careers.

Melba Pattillo Beals

Melba Pattillo Beals received a bachelor's degree from San Francisco State University and a master's in communications from Columbia University. In 2009, she earned her PhD in education from the University of San Francisco. Melba has worked as a journalist for NBC and is the author of *Warriors Don't Cry: A Searing Memoir of the Battle to Integrate Little Rock's Central High*. A public speaker by nature, she often makes appearances to speak about the crisis.

Elizabeth Eckford

After completing her high school requirements, Elizabeth Eckford joined the US Army. She attended Central State University in Wilberforce, Ohio, and returned to Little Rock in her thirties. Still shaken by her experiences, she avoided talking about the 1957 high school year until 1996. Now she talks with young people about the crisis as a way to promote healing. She is on the board of directors for the Central High Museum and Visitor Center and was recently working as a probation officer.

Ernest Green

Ernest Green received his master's degree in sociology from Michigan State University. He was the assistant Secretary of Housing and Urban Affairs during President Jimmy Carter's administration from 1977 to 1981. Green worked as Managing Director at Lehman Brothers in Washington, DC, and served on the boards of the NAACP and the Winthrop Rockefeller Foundation.

Gloria Ray Karlmark

Gloria Ray Karlmark moved to Missouri and graduated from the Kansas City Central High School. She graduated with bachelor degrees in chemistry and mathematics from the Illinois Institute of Technology. Gloria has held jobs in countries around the world. She became a patent attorney in Sweden in 1977. She worked as a documentation specialist in Belgium and became the editor-in-chief for an international journal on computers in industry.

Carlotta Walls LaNier

Carlotta Walls LaNier graduated from Central High in 1960. She holds a bachelor of science degree from Colorado State. She worked with teenagers at the YMCA before founding a real estate brokerage firm.

Terrence Roberts

Terrence Roberts earned a bachelor's degree in sociology, a master's degree in social welfare, and a PhD in psychology. He has worked in hospitals and was the department chair at Antioch University until starting a management-consulting firm. Terrence published his memoir, *Lessons From Little Rock*, in 2009, and a second book, *Simple Not Easy*, in 2010. Terrence continues to lecture about the Little Rock crisis around the country.

Jefferson Thomas

Jefferson Thomas graduated from Central High School in 1960. Drafted into the Army, he served his country again in Vietnam. He received his college degree from California State University in Los Angeles. He was an accountant for the United States Department of Defense and until he retired in 2004. Jefferson died of pancreatic cancer in 2010.

Minnijean Brown Trickey

Minnijean Brown Trickey graduated from New York's New Lincoln School in 1959. She attended Southern Illinois University, then moved to Canada where she received a master's of social work degree from Carleton University in Ontario and raised six children. She moved back to Arkansas in 2003. She is a social activist and lectures at colleges around the country.

Thelma Mothershed-Wair

During the year without school, Thelma Mothershed-Wair took correspondence courses and attended summer school. She received her Central High School diploma by mail. Thelma earned her master's degree in guidance and counseling from Southern Illinois University. She taught home economics for twenty-eight years before retiring in 1994.

CHAPTER NOTES

Chapter 1. The First Morning

1. Carlotta Walls LaNier, *A Mighty Long Way* (New York: Random House, 2009), 70.
2. Taylor Branch, *The King Years: Historic Moments in the Civil Rights Movement* (New York: Simon & Schuster, 2013), 6.
3. Elizabeth Jacoway, *Turn Away Thy Son: Little Rock, The Crisis that Shocked the Nation* (New York: Free Press, 2007), 4.
4. Daisy Bates, *The Long Shadow of Little Rock* (Fayetteville, Ark.: University of Arkansas Press, 1986), 75.
5. Ibid., 70.
6. Ibid., 75.
7. Ibid., 70.
8. Melba Pattillo Beals, *Warriors Don't Cry* (New York: Simon & Schuster, 2007), 37.

Chapter 2. The Fight for Equality in the Schools

1. Eric Foner, "The Meaning of Freedom," *Reconstruction* (New York: HarperCollins, 1988), http://www.njstatelib.org/research_library/new_jersey_resources/digital_collection/unfinished_revolution.
2. National Historic Landmark Survey, "Racial Desegregation in Public Education in the United States Theme Study," *National Register, History and Education Program National Park Service Department of the Interior*, Washington, D.C., 2000, 10.
3. Ibid., 12.
4. Roy Wilkins with Tom Mathews, *Standing Fast: The Autobiography of Roy Wilkins* (New York: De Capo Press, 1994), 234.
5. "Introduction to the Court Opinion on the *Plessy* v. *Ferguson* Case," Source 163 U.S. 537 (1896), *US Department of State*, accessed February 14, 2015, http://www.ait.org.tw/infousa/zhtw/DOCS/basic_reading/33.html.
6. Ibid.
7. National Historic Landmark Survey, 74.
8. Thurgood Marshall, *His Speeches, Writings, Arguments, Opinions, and Reminiscences*, ed. Mark V. Tushnet (Chicago: Lawrence Hill Books, 2001), 156.

9. Howard Ball, *A Defiant Life: Thurgood Marshall and the Persistence of Racism in America* (New York: Crown Publishers, 1998), 123.
10. Ibid., 17.
11. *Brown v. Board of Education*, 347 U.S. 483 (1954), The National Center for Public Policy Research, accessed February 14, 2015, http://www.nationalcenter.org/brown.html.

Chapter 3. The Little Rock Nine

1. Melba Pattillo Beals, *Warriors Don't Cry* (New York: HarperCollins, 2007), 27
2. Elizabeth Jacoway, *Turn Away Thy Son: Little Rock, The Crisis that Shocked the Nation* (New York: Free Press, 2007), 101.
3. Ibid., 105.
4. Daisy Bates, *The Long Shadow of Little Rock* (Fayetteville, Ark.: University of Arkansas Press, 1986), 133.
5. Jacoway, 103.
6. Beals, 41.
7. Ibid., 27.
8. Bates, 122.
9. Ibid., 130.
10. Ibid., 131.

Chapter 4. Calling In the Troops

1. Daisy Bates, *The Long Shadow of Little Rock* (Fayetteville, Ark.: University of Arkansas Press, 1986), 4.
2. Elizabeth Jacoway, *Turn Away Thy Son: Little Rock, The Crisis that Shocked the Nation* (New York: Free Press, 2007), 73.
3. Bates, 57.
4. Ibid., 8.
5. Ibid, 57.
6. Ibid., 60.
7. Ibid., 61.
8. Benjamin Fine, "Militia Sent to Little Rock; School Integration Put Off," *Little Rock: 40 Years Later, New York Times Learning Network,* 1997, http://events.nytimes.com/learning/general/specials/littlerock/090357ds-militia.html.
9. Melba Pattillo Beals, *Warriors Don't Cry* (New York: Washington Square Press, 1994), 39.
10. Ibid.

11. Ibid.
12. Bates, 61.
13. Ibid., 63.
14. Ibid., 64.
15. Dwight D. Eisenhower, "Letter, DDE to Swede Hazlett, boyhood friend, Captain, USN, July 22, 1957," *Dwight D. Eisenhower Presidential Library, Museum and Boyhood Home*, accessed January 31, 2015, http://www.eisenhower.archives. gov/research/online_documents/civil_rights_brown_v_boe/ 1957_07_22_DDE_to_Hazlett.pdf.
16. Dwight D. Eisenhower, "Diary notes DDE re mtg with Faubus," *Dwight D. Eisenhower Presidential Library, Museum and Boyhood Home*, accessed February 14, 2015, http://eisenhower. archives.gov/research/online_documents/civil_rights_little_ rock/1957_10_08_Diary_Notes_Faubus_Meeting.pdf.
17. Ibid.
18. Beals, 93.
19. Bates, 92.
20. Carlotta Walls LaNeir, "A Mighty Long Way," (New York: Random House, 2009), 89.
21. Bates, 93.
22. Woodrow Wilson Mann, "Telegram Woodrow Wilson Mann to President Eisenhower, September 24, 1957," *Dwight D. Eisenhower Presidential Library, Museum and Boyhood Home*, accessed January 31, 2015, http://www.eisenhower.archives. gov/research/online_documents/civil_rights_little_rock/1957 _09_24_Mann_to_DDE.pdf.
23. "Ike on Little Rock," *American Radioworks*, accessed February 14, 2015, http://americanradioworks.publicradio.org/features/ marshall/ike.html.
24. Dwight D. Eisenhower, "Letter, President Eisenhower to Jackie Robinson, June 4, 1958," *Dwight D. Eisenhower Presidential Library, Museum and Boyhood Home*, accessed February 14, 2015, http://eisenhower.archives.gov/research/ online_documents/civil_rights_little_rock/1958_06_04_ DDE_to_Robinson.pdf.
25. Bates, 104.
26. Ibid., 106.

Chapter 5. Stormy Days at Central High

1. Andrea Stone, "In Little Rock, a small act of defiance endures," *USA Today*, August 30, 2007, http://usatoday30.usatoday.com/news/nation/2007-08-29-Littlerock_N.htm.
2. Georgia Dortch and Jane Emery "The Price We Pay," *The Tiger*: Little Rock Central High School, October 3, 1957, http://www.ncdemocracy.org/sites/www.ncdemocracy.org/files/docs/NDEP-LittleRock-STUDENT_EDITORIALS.pdf.
3. "Let's Keep the Record Straight," *The Tiger*: *Little Rock Central High School Paper*, October 3, 1957, http://www.ncdemocracy.org/sites/www.ncdemocracy.org/files/docs/NDEP-LittleRock-STUDENT_EDITORIALS.pdf.
4. Carlotta Walls LaNier, *A Mighty Long Way*, (New York: Random House, 2009), 100.
5. Melba Pattillo Beals, *Warriors Don't Cry* (New York: Harper-Collins, 2007), 121.
6. Elizabeth Huckaby, *Crisis at Central High, Little Rock, 1957–1958* (Baton Rouge, La.: Louisiana State University Press, 1980), 52.
7. Daisy Bates, *The Long Shadow of Little Rock* (Fayetteville, Ark.: University of Arkansas Press, 1986), 126.
8. Huckaby, 85.
9. Elizabeth Jacoway, *Turn Away Thy Son: Little Rock, The Crisis that Shocked the Nation* (New York: Free Press, 2007), 194.
10. "Little Rock Central High School: The Little Rock Nine," National Park Service, *US Department of the Interior*, accessed February 14, 2015, http://www.nps.gov/chsc/planyourvisit/upload/Site-Bulletin-Little-Rock-Nine.pdf.
11. Huckaby, 93.
12. Ibid., 149.
13. Ibid., 152.
14. Ibid.
15. Huckaby, 159.

Chapter 6. Attacks and Threats Hit Home

1. Elizabeth Jacoway, *Turn Away Thy Son: Little Rock, The Crisis that Shocked the Nation* (New York: Free Press, 2007), 229.
2. Melba Pattillo Beals, *Warriors Don't Cry* (New York: Simon & Schuster, 2007), 159.

3. Daisy Bates, *The Long Shadow of Little Rock* (Fayetteville, Ark.: University of Arkansas Press, 1986), 171.
4. Beals, 205.

Chapter 7. Graduation Time

1. Carlotta Walls LaNier, *A Mighty Long Way* (New York: Random House, 2007), 128.
2. Melba Pattillo Beals, *Warriors Don't Cry* (New York: Washington Square Press, 1994), 212.
3. Ibid, 211.
4. Ernest Green, "Ernest Green Describes Experience at Central High," *Old State House Museum: The Arkansas News*, 2007, http://www.oldstatehouse.com/collections/classroom/arkansas_news.aspx?issue=5&page=4&detail=46.
5. Elizabeth Huckaby, *Crisis at Central High, Little Rock, 1957–1958* (Baton Rouge, La.: Louisiana State University Press, 1980), 208.
6. Ibid., 210.

Chapter 8. The Year the Schools Closed

1. "Crisis Timeline," National Park Service, *US Department of the Interior*, July 25, 2006, http://www.nps.gov/chsc/history culture/timeline.htm.
2. Elizabeth Jacoway, *Understanding the Little Rock Crisis: An Exercise in Remembrance and Reconciliation* (Fayetteville, Ark.: University of Arkansas Press, 1999), 11.
3. Andrew A. Green, "Little Rock's 'Lost Class' of 1959 recalls turbulent year," *Arkansas Democrat-Gazette*, 1998, http://www.ardemgaz.com/prev/central/acclass27.html.
4. *Cooper et al.* v. *Aaron et al*, 358 U.S. 1958.
5. Mary Peterson, interview with author, August 2006.
6. Melba Pattillo Beals, *Warriors Don't Cry* (New York: Simon & Schuster, 2007), 219.
7. Andrew A. Green.
8. Ibid.

Chapter 9. Progress and Promise

1. Bill Clinton, "One America for today, tomorrow and forever, Clinton says," *Arkansas Online*, September 25, 1997, http://www.arkansasonline.com/news/1997/sep/25/one-america-

today-tomorrow-and-forever-clinton-say/?news-arkansas-specials-central_crisis.

2. Ibid.
3. United Press International, "1957's 'Little Rock Nine' Return to Central High in Joy, Sadness," *Los Angeles Times*, October 23, 1987, http://articles.latimes.com/1987-10-23/news/mn-10813_1_central-high.
4. Elizabeth Jacoway, *Understanding the Little Rock Crisis: An Exercise in Remembrance and Reconciliation*, eds., Elizabeth Jacoway and C. Fred Williams (Fayetteville, Ark.: University of Arkansas Press, 1999), 20–21.
5. Kevin Sack, "In Little Rock, Clinton Warns of Racial Split," *The New York Times*, September 26, 1997, A1.
6. P. J. Reilly, "'We Just Wanted To Go To School': Minnijean Brown-Trickey, One of the Little Rock Nine Still Fighting Racism," *Intelligencer Journal*, Lancaster, Pa., January 23, 2003, 1.
7. Kate Taylor, "Students Invite Real-Life Lesson in History," *The Oregonian*, Portland, Ore., March 17, 2004, C.01.
8. *Tulsa World*, "Clinton Greets Famed Little Rock Nine/ Today, Former Students Welcomed Among Cheers," *Tulsa World*, Tulsa, Okla., September 26, 1997, A6.
9. David Hammer, "Little Rock Statue Unveiled/New Monument Shows the Group in its Defiant Walk to First Day of School with Whites in '57," *Houston Chronicle*, Houston Tex., August 31, 2005, 03.
10. Bill Clinton, "One America for today, tomorrow and forever, Clinton says," *Arkansas Online*, September 25, 1997, http://www.arkansasonline.com/news/1997/sep/25/one-america-today-tomorrow-and-forever-clinton-say/?news-arkansas-specials-central_crisis.
11. "Central High School," accessed February 9, 2015, http://www.publicschoolreview.com/school_ov/school_id/4283.
12. "Mapping the Road to Change: Insights on Perception, Prejudice and Acceptance," *Little Rock Central High.net*, accessed February 9, 2015, http://www.lrcentralhigh.net/memory.html.
13. Clinton.

TIMELINE

1954   *May 17*—The US Supreme Court rules on the *Brown* v. *Board of Education* case, saying the doctrine of "separate but equal" has no place in public education.

May 22—The Little Rock school board says it will comply with the Supreme Court ruling.

1957   *August 27*—A member of the Mothers' League of Central High School files a lawsuit asking a federal court to postpone the integration.

August 30—Federal District Judge Ronald Davies rules that the integration must begin as planned.

September 2—Governor Orval Faubus calls out the Arkansas National Guard to surround Little Rock Central High School and addresses the state.

September 3—Judge Davies , believing that the Guard has been called to protect people and property, tells the NAACP to continue the planned integration.

September 4—Elizabeth Eckford faces the angry mob alone and is stopped from entering the school by the National Guard; the other African-American students walking with ministers are also turned away.

September 20—Judge Davies forbids Governor Faubus from further interference.

September 23—The nine African-American students enter Central High through a side door; the angry mob attacks three African-American reporters; the nine students are removed from school for their protection.

September 24—President Eisenhower announces he is sending troops to carry out the court order.

September 25—The 101st Airborne Division escorts the nine African-American students into Central High.

December—After months of abuse by white students, Minnijean Brown drops food on two boys who are blocking her way; she is suspended for six days.

1958 *February 6*—After more harassment by white students, Minnijean is expelled from Central High for retaliating.

May 27—Ernest Green becomes the first African-American student to receive a diploma from Central High.

June 21—Federal District Judge Harry Lemley grants a three-year delay of integration that the school board has requested; the NAACP appeals.

August—Governor Faubus asks the state legislature to pass a law allowing him to close public schools to avoid integration; the legislature overwhelmingly passes the bill.

August 18—The Eighth Circuit Court of Appeals in St. Louis reverses Judge Lemley's ruling but grants the school board time for an appeal to the Supreme Court.

September 12—The Supreme Court rules that Little Rock must continue with its integration plan. The school board announces that school will begin in three days; Governor Faubus uses the new law and closes all of Little Rock's high schools.

September 27—Residents vote to keep the schools closed.

December 6—A new school board is elected; three members want to continue the integration; three members are segregationist and want to resist the court order.

1959 *May 5*—Those against segregation on the school board walk out of a meeting in protest; the three remaining segregationist members fire forty-four faculty who support integration.

May 25—Voters decide to remove the segregationist members from the school board; they also decide to keep the moderate members.

June 18—The school-closing law is ruled unconstitutional; school is scheduled for the following fall.

August 12—The school board opens public high schools a month early.

1972	All grades in Little Rock public schools are fully integrated.
1997	The fortieth anniversary of the integration of Central High School on September 26.
2006	Two members of the Little Rock Nine help break ground for a new museum and visitor's center on May 20.
2007	Celebrating the fiftieth anniversary of Central High's desegregation, the National Park Service formally dedicates the new visitor center on September 24.
2009	The Little Rock Nine are invited by Barack Obama to attend his presidential inauguration on January 20. All but two attend.

GLOSSARY

appeal—To ask a higher court to review a lower court's decision.

civil disobedience—Deliberate breaking of the law carried out as a nonviolent protest.

commencement—A graduation ceremony during which diplomas are given.

conscience—An internal sense of what is right and wrong.

desegregation—The ending of enforced separation of ethnic or racial groups.

discrimination—Unfair treatment of a person or group based on prejudice.

injunction—A legal order that requires somebody to do or refrain from doing something.

integration—The process of opening a group, place, or organization to all people.

ordinance—A rule or law made by an authority such as a government.

prejudice—An unfounded hatred, fear, or mistrust of a person or group, usually with regard to a particular religion, race, ethnicity, nationality, or social status.

progressive—Advocating social, economic, or political reform.

provocation—An act designed to make somebody angry or upset.

scholarship—A sum of money awarded to help a student pay for education expenses.

segregation—Separation; often used to describe a practice of keeping ethnic, racial, or gender groups separate.

sit-in—A form of protest in which people occupy a place and refuse to leave until their demands are met.

FURTHER READING

Books

Bausum, Ann. *Marching to the Mountaintop.* Washington, D.C.: National Geographic. 2012.

Higgins, Nadia. *The Split History of the Civil Rights Movement.* Mankato, Minn: Compass Point, 2014.

Hunter-Gault, Charlayne. *To the Mountaintop: My Journey Through the Civil Rights Movement.* Flash Point, 2012.

Magoon, Kekla. *Today the World Is Watching You: The Little Rock Nine and the Fight for School Integration, 1957.* Minneapolis: Twenty-First Century, 2011.

Osborne, Linda Barrett. *Miles to Go for Freedom.* New York: Harry N. Abrams, 2012.

Tougas, Shelley. *Little Rock Girl 1957: How a Photograph Changed the Fight for Integration.* Mankato, Minn.: Compass Point Books, 2011.

Web Sites

memory.loc.gov/ammem/aaohtml/exhibit/aopart9.html
Covers major civil rights milestones, includes photos and original documents.

life.time.com/history/little-rock-nine-1957-photos
A Life magazine restrospective of the Little Rock crisis through photos.

pbs.org/wgbh/amex/eyesontheprize/story/03_schools.html
Explains the school desegregation movement with background information, photos, and video.

INDEX